The Church —
Subtly Deceived?

The Church —
Subtly Deceived?

Alexander Seibel

Published by
THE OLIVE PRESS
Midnight Call, Inc.
Columbia, South Carolina U.S.A.

Printed in the United States of America

ISBN 1-85307-108-1

Published by The Olive Press, a division of Midnight Call Ministries,
West Columbia, SC 29170 U.S.A.
(Cover by J Spurling)

Library of Congress Cataloging-in-Publication Data

Seibel, Alexander
    The Church: Subtly Deceived?
    ISBN 1-85307-108-1
    1. Bible—Tongues—Passivity—Signs   2. Ecumenism

Printed in the United States of America

CONTENTS

PUBLISHER'S NOTE

This book has been prepared to make available a selection of the vital writings of Alexander Seibel of Germany. All the contents are taken from his book, *The Church Infiltrated* (September 1984), and from two papers by the same author entitled, "The Charismatic Movement, a Biblical Perspective of Signs and Wonders," and "The Spirit of Truth and the Spirit of Error."

Scripture quotations are taken from the Authorized Version (Crown Copyright), unless otherwise stated.

PREFACE

My initial contact with the author of this book represents one of the most striking encounters of my Christian service. Obviously Evangelist Seibel has experienced considerable distress concerning the undermining of the church in these last days. As Christians, many of us share this same distress.

The subject is one of pressing importance. Several times the New Testament makes reference to the danger of a Christian being undermined by the powers of darkness in the last days.

Now this is contrary to the widespread opinion of many believers who claim that such a thing is not written in the Bible anywhere. The Apostle warns his hearers at Corinth that Satan could defraud them. In 2nd Corinthians 11:4, Paul highlights the danger that believers can in fact "receive another spirit, which ye have not received." According to 1st Timothy 4, the influence of evil spirits in the church itself and among believers will increase in the latter times.

In the light of these warnings from the Word of God, it will be necessary to test especially those much-praised Pentecostal and Charismatic movements of this century. Alexander Seibel clearly sees this as part of his special commission. His warning call is alarming and at times provocative.

It would certainly have been easier for him to write against obvious heresies, modernistic Bible criticism, and so on. However, he has set out in this work to bring to light some of the evangelically-disguised moves of the adversary of God.

The undermining work of the enemy in the endtimes is commonly confused with the edifying work of our Lord Jesus Christ. Christians must learn to detect these things and take care to avoid them. It is our desire and our prayer that this publication will be used of God to this end.

Peter Mayer
Bible School, Beatenberg
(From Preface to *The Church Infiltrated*)

SIGNS OF THE TIMES

Most of us, today, are convinced that we are living at a time just preceding the Second Coming of the Lord Jesus.

We should, therefore, not really be surprised by the events we see. All these things have been predicted with great accuracy in the Holy Scriptures.

The age in which we live is often disturbed by unusual events. There are many spiritual currents and much that is characterized by confusion and deception.

We should note that the Lord Jesus repeatedly introduces the subject of His coming again in the Gospels (Matthew 24, Mark 13, Luke 21) with DECEPTION: "...take heed that no one leads you astray" (Matthew 24:4). Hence, we are called to extraordinary watchfulness, which the Lord, who rarely repeats Himself, has particularly admonished us to have.

In the last five verses of Mark 13, the Lord repeats, "be watchful" four times: His last sentence is, "And what I say unto you I say unto all, Watch." If the Lord particularly warned us of deception and called us to vigilance, we cannot hope to live the Christian life in an indifferent fashion, lacking in watchfulness, without rebuke from the Lord. In view of this, there are many things that we need to consider very carefully lest we be misled.

The Charismatic Movement draws a parallel between modern visible phenomena and the early church with its signs and wonders. The Book of Acts seems, at first sight, to deliver an adequate basis for this, but on closer examination is it, by itself, a sufficiently Biblical basis?

It is vital to note that the sections of the Scriptures dealing with the return of our Lord Jesus emphasize the area of deception, whether they be speeches of our Lord Jesus, or letters of the apostles. In these sections, signs and wonders are repeatedly mentioned, but not in a positive context. Instead, warning is given concerning them and their function of deception.

The comment of our Lord Jesus in Matthew 24:24 is, "For there shall arise false Christs, and false prophets, and shall shew great signs and wonders; insomuch that, if it were possible, they shall deceive the very elect." In a similar way, Paul writes in 2nd Thessalonians 2:9, "…the working of Satan with all power and signs and lying wonders."

Therefore, it is imperative that we read those sections of the Bible which deal with our generation if we wish to understand current events. The Acts of the Apostles (beginning of the church) does not describe our time.

The classic epistle dealing with this present era is 2nd Thessalonians. Here, Paul, in harmony with the ministry of Christ relative to His coming again, says in chapter 2, verse 3: "Let no man deceive you by any means; for that day shall not come, except there be a falling away first…." First, the apostasy — not the world-wide revival — as is so often intimated by these movements which place great emphasis on supernatural signs.

The Bible speaks of the opposite — the great apostasy. The Lord Jesus says, "…Nevertheless, when the Son of Man cometh, shall He find faith on the Earth?" (Luke 18:8). Also, He compares the days preceding His coming again with the days of Noah, "But, as the days of Noah were, so shall also the coming of the Son of Man be" (Matthew 24:37).

When we read Genesis 6, we catch a glimpse of a universal collapse, "…for all flesh had corrupted his way upon the Earth" (Genesis 6:12). In a similar way, the comment in 2nd Thessalonians 2:3 should be understood: "…there comes a falling away first…that the man of sin be revealed…." Here, in the original Greek, we have the word "anomia," which simply means "lawlessness."

We must reckon with unheard-of anarchy, increases in violence and unprecedented lawlessness prior to the coming again of Jesus Christ.

During these dark days in which terror, dissolution of order and God's laws, and violence are on the increase, we must expect, according to 2nd Thessalonians 2:9–11, the appearance of movements which emphasize signs and wonders in a previously unheard-of fashion. Paul then continues in 2nd Thessalonians 2, verse 4: "…Who opposeth and exalteth himself above all that is called God, or that is worshipped; so that he as God sitteth in the Temple of God, shewing himself that he is God."

Here is something else worthy of note. Many commentators understand that prior to the return of Jesus, the Temple in Jerusalem will be rebuilt, in which the Antichrist will then sit and demand worship. This is quite possible and I, personally, have no difficulty in believing that this will be literally fulfilled.

Despite this, I think this reference has at least one other possible interpretation, which is supported by reading the five other Bible references in which Paul talks about the Temple of God. We must add that when the Lord Jesus talks about the visible Temple buildings (Matthew 21:12), the Greek word used is "heiron." In the Pauline epistles, the Greek word for Temple is always "naos," which really means "holy" or "holy of holies."

This is the word used in 1st Corinthians 3:16–17 where Paul says, "Know ye not that ye are the Temple of God, and that the Spirit of God dwelleth in you? If any man defile the Temple of God, him shall God destroy; for the Temple of God is holy, which Temple ye are."

Here we always have the Greek word "naos" for the Temple, as in 1st Corinthians 6:16 and Ephesians 2:21. In these five passages, the Temple of God always refers to the church or individual believers. The same word, "naos," is used in 2nd Thessalonians 2:4.

The Antichrist, this anti-Christian spirit, seats himself in the "naos," in God's Temple. Thus, before the return of Christ, we must expect an incredibly comprehensive infiltration of the churches and believers, as we can see in a growing penetration of liberalism, modernism, ecumenism and mysticism right before our eyes.

Many speak of great outpourings of the Spirit and revivals today.

However, one glance at the world brings one face-to-face with reality. The terror, confusion, chaos, brutality, sexual liberation and demonic perversion are raging like a torrent. Anarchism is spreading. Human life is worth less and less. Vicious murders, kidnapping, blackmail and even Satanism are increasing at an alarming rate.

The prevailing conditions in the world are in a certain sense a barometer for the spiritual effectiveness of the believers who are the salt of the Earth.

Consequently, anyone claiming to witness a revival in our day would seem to be sadly blinded (Revelation 3: 17–18). Such blindness is in itself an indication of the judgment of God (Isaiah 29:9–10, Psalm 69:23 et cetera).

Instead of a world-wide revival before us, we have a satanic Pentecost before us which is being masterminded by the powers of anarchy and confusion.

Let us think for a moment of the conflicts in the visible world: One fights without official declarations of war, conquers countries without official battles, one undermines and sabotages the enemy, infiltrates the battle lines which are becoming more and more confused, one smiles in a friendly manner at a conference and then kills in an ambush, ideology intersperses the armies in such a way that one does not know who is a friend or foe.

In my opinion, this shows us to a certain degree what is going on in the invisible battlefronts. It is a horrible strategy which brings the enemy into the ranks of God's children, and is intended to disturb them, divide them and turn them against each other. The sins of lukewarmness and compromise successfully open the doors to our enemies.

There is a parallel with the people of Israel who believed themselves to be very spiritual, yet the prophets compared them with Sodom and Gomorrah (Isaiah 1:10).

May the Lord bring His church to the cross anew, for without repentance there is no victory. Watchman Nee writes in his book, *The Latent Power of the Soul*:

> All who have spiritual insight and sensitivity know the reality of this statement. Soul power is rushing toward us like a torrent, making use of science (psychology and parapsychology), religion, and even an ignorant church (in her seeking excessively supernatural manifestations and in her not controlling supernatural gifts according to the guidance of the Bible), Satan is causing this world to filled with the power of darkness.
>
> Yet this is but Satan's last and final preparation for the manifestation of the Antichrist.
>
> Those who are truly spiritual (that is, those who reject soul power) sense all around them the acceleration of opposition from the evil spirits. The whole atmosphere is so darkened that they find it hard to advance. [1]

Praying believers alone are still able to hold back the judgement.

Today, we also observe the increasing tendency toward creating the "right mood." This is cultivated through various emotional and worldly actions and techniques such as rhythm, hard beat, clapping, shouting, sighing, et cetera.

Such an atmosphere is supposed to indicate "life" and "fullness of the spirit."

To members of dead churches, particularly, such "lively meetings" have a special appeal, but unfortunately, emotional excitement is often confused with the genuine work of the Holy Spirit. The Holy Spirit causes feelings, but feelings don't bring about the Holy Spirit.

NINE MATTERS FOR SERIOUS CONSIDERATION

When considering the Charismatic Movement, heated discussion is often generated as to the value of tongue-speaking, as if this were the only characteristic. There are almost as many opinions about tongue-speaking as there are people who write books about it. Yet, this movement has other accompanying symptoms which we must examine in the light of God's Word.

Point 1

SPIRIT BAPTISM

One of the marks of this movement is, with a few exceptions, the exegetically untenable interpretation of Spirit baptism as an experience separate from conversion.

Verse 13 of 1st Corinthians 12 tells us explicitly that we are all baptized by one Spirit. The exact [Greek] grammatical form is: passive, indicative, aorist (past) — once and for all it was accomplished at regeneration.

The word "all" includes not only spiritual, but also carnal Christians. They have ALL been made to drink into one Spirit. This ALL stands in contrast to verse 30, where the Apostle asks, "...Do all speak with tongues? Do all interpret?" To each of these questions a clear NO is expected. These passages express clearly that baptism of the Spirit and the speaking of tongues are two different things.

The term "baptized with the Spirit or Holy Ghost" actually occurs seven times in the Bible, once in an epistle (the above quoted verse from 1st Corinthians), four times in the Gospels (Matthew 3:11; Mark 1:8; Luke 3:16 and John 1:33) and twice in the Book of Acts (1:5; 11:16). Let us note that verses 14–16 of Acts 11 tell us that the baptism of the Spirit and the salvation of Cornelius were identical.

Passages in the Book of Acts have been the main cause of considerable confusion and controversy about this subject. Therefore we wish to quote here from Alfred Kuen to clarify this important issue. Concerning this critical area he makes several important statements:

> If we believe that the Holy Spirit teaches the Truth in the
> Word of God then we must obtain our doctrines purely and
> simply from the Word of God and must make our expression
> conform to those used by the inspired authors of the Bible.
> Therefore when we speak of "receiving of the Spirit," of
> "baptism of the Spirit," and of "filling of the Spirit," we must
> use the same expressions and use them in the same sense as

the Bible does. This is not merely a matter of strife over words. Words are bearers of spiritual realities and events and the history of recent decades provides abundant proof that blithely changing one word for another leads to spiritual confusion.

The well-known revivalist Charles Finney, for instance, described one special experience of his Christian life as "Baptism of Power." His friend and colleague in the school of Oberlin, Asa Mahan, named this experience: "Baptism of the Spirit." The evangelist Reuben Torrey took up this concept and systematically dealt with it in his book, *Baptism of the Spirit.* Torrey suggests that this is a special experience which the believer can have after conversion and that it equips him with special power from on high and gifts of the Spirit for Christian service.

The founders of the Pentecostal Movement received Torrey's interpretation and added one further point: The sign of having received the baptism of the Spirit, they claimed, was speaking in tongues. Thus we have here the emergence of a doctrine which has been accepted by millions of Christians throughout the world today.

Before one accepts any doctrine, how necessary it is to examine that doctrine in order to determine whether it originates in the Word of God or in some historical development of dogmatism!

In asking oneself, "What does the Bible teach?" one must be willing to abandon the kinds of methods unfortunately found in so many Christian circles where personal assumptions are allowed to override the Word of God. Any statement one makes concerning doctrine must have basis in the Word of God.

It is commonly claimed today that one must be converted and then later, through a second experience, one may receive the Holy Spirit or the baptism of the Spirit. As proof of this, the apostles who received the Holy Spirit at Pentecost are cited, along with the Samaritans, the disciples at Ephesus and eventually also the Apostle Paul. Thousands of conversions referred to in the Book of Acts are neglected in the process. Instances where believers immediately received the Holy Spirit — without the laying on of hands and without the speaking in tongues — are not mentioned at all. Attention is never drawn to the fact that the apostles never encouraged anyone in any of the epistles to seek or to wait for such a second experience or baptism of the Spirit.

If one really wants to know what the Bible teaches, then one must be willing to use the same inductive method employed by scientists in their research of the laws of nature. One must proceed from what the Bible says and from there, draw one's conclusions, but only after one has honestly examined everything Scripture teaches on the subject.

If one wishes to know what the apostles taught, one must first examine their thoughts in the epistles.

This means one must read the epistles and accept the conclusions drawn from these letters. Then, one must apply them to the Gospels and the Book of Acts — not the other way round. The Gospels and the Book of Acts inform us of a solitary, never-to-be-repeated series of acts in history.

These include how the Word became flesh; how the Lord Jesus suffered for us; His resurrection on the third day; how He ascended into heaven and how ten days later; He poured out the Holy Spirit on His disciples.

Like Christ's crucifixion and Easter Sunday, Pentecost cannot be repeated. To pray for a new Pentecost makes just as little sense as asking for a new incarnation of the Lord Jesus Christ.

Those who now enjoy God's unique salvation live in a new dispensation and not in a period of transition. The Scripture teaches that no one is called to move through such a transitional period as did the apostles who moved from the old Covenant to the New.

In the epistles, we discover the truth of the New Covenant and the baptism of the Holy Spirit is the first step in the believer's life. We are buried with Christ by baptism into His death and with Him are raised up into newness of life in order to become members of Christ's body. [2]

The teaching that the baptism of the Holy Spirit is a second or special experience connected with holiness is not Biblical.

The Scriptures do not teach us anywhere that we are to ask God or the Lord Jesus for a Spirit baptism. The apostles do not encourage or exhort us in any of their letters to seek a spirit baptism or a "second experience." As pointed out before, in 1st Corinthians 12:13, the emphasis lies on the word "all." That, which is the basis for the unity of all believers in the Scriptures, is used as the ground for distinction, discrimination and separation. No wonder the body of Christ suffers so many outward divisions!

Although George Mallone speaks in tongues himself and comes out in favor of these special gifts, yet he has to admit in his book, *Those Controversial Gifts*, when dealing with tongues, that they are "...the biggest Christian friendship and oneness buster of the century."

The Bible does indeed know two kinds of believers, but not charismatics or non-charismatics, nor those being baptized in the Spirit or those not baptized, but rather carnal (1st Corinthians 3:1–3) and spiritual Christians (1st Corinthians 2:15). The change from carnal to spiritual is not the reception of special gifts, but usually repentance.

This doctrine of the special baptism of the Spirit is practically the basis of the whole Pentecostal Movement. Again, the simplest architectural information is sufficient for us to realize that the most beautiful and impressive building cannot stand on the wrong foundation. The inconsistency of some believers over this point has often astonished me. Many are shown to be dazzled by the growing superstructure. One gets the impression that a mistake greatly multiplied cannot be a mistake anymore.

It is something different; however, when the Bible speaks about being filled with the Holy Spirit. The expression "full of the Holy Spirit" or "filled with the Holy Spirit" occurs fourteen times in the Gospels and the Book of Acts, and interestingly only once in the epistles (Ephesians 5:18). This filling does not take place once for all, but is a matter of daily surrender and dying to self as one accepts the cross. Holiness and the cross are inseparable. This is why we read again and again of this process (Acts 2:4, 4:8, 4:31 and so on).

It should be noted that some authors speak about a "baptism of the Holy Spirit" but really mean a "filling of the Holy Spirit." It should also be noted that there is no case of anyone receiving the "baptism of the Holy Spirit" after having received the Holy Spirit.

Point 2

GIFTS

The movement is marked by a wrong emphasis on certain gifts, especially those with sign character — foremost among them tongues. Here, the *last* Biblical gift has been put *first*.

A. Tongues for private edification?

The gift of tongues is only mentioned in one epistle —in 1st Corinthians. Paul wrote this letter for a specific church situation which was marked by a terrible mixture of light and darkness and it contains primarily instruction, corrections, explanations and reproofs. The church was in a highly deplorable and unspiritual condition.

The believers, through their conceit and pride, "super-spirituality" and sins, caused the apostle much grief, sorrow and heartache (2nd Corinthians 2:4); a rather sad if not discouraging fact then as well as today.

The Christians at Corinth are encouraged in this 14th chapter to seek after prophecy and not after an unknown tongue. Beginning at verse 2, Paul gives the reason why prophecy is the greater of these two gifts. "I would rather that ye prophesy, for..." (14:1–2).

Then he brings forward arguments against the overemphasized use of tongues, as was obviously the case in Corinth, and at the same time, reasons for the use of prophecy. Really he is saying: "When you speak in tongues no one can understand you except God. But when you prophesy, you edify and exhort others. When you speak in tongues, you only edify yourselves; but when you prophesy, you edify the church." These are convincing reasons why prophecy presents the more desirable gift. The emphasis lies on the word 'but' in verse four as well as verse five, "...but rather that ye prophesied."

According to Numbers 11:29, prophets were people upon whom the Lord put His Spirit, and it was through the prophet that the will of God was revealed.

We are exhorted to heed the prophetic Word (2nd Peter 1:19) and to desire the sincere milk (1st Peter 2:2) which is the Word of God. We are promised that we may become mature through an intimate acquaintance with the Scriptures and the obedience connected with it (2nd Timothy 3:16).

Significantly, it does not say anywhere that we may become mature through "special" gifts or their use.

Now it is clearly visible that the Spirit of God identifies Himself with His Word. "The words I have spoken to you are spirit and they are life," declares the Lord Jesus (John 6 :63). Michael Griffiths writes:

> According to 1st Corinthians 14:5, prophecy refers to the commonest and most edifying type of speaking in the assembly. This indeed has been the traditional evangelical understanding. The New Testament usage conforms far more to the Old Testament usage of a fearless proclamation of the Word of God expounded in the light of the contemporary situation.[3]

One should not be too dogmatic here, yet Spiros Zodhiates' statement about the same subject is noteworthy:

> Paul uses the term in its widest sense as the speaking forth of the Word of God and in the narrower sense of revealing the future. Who are prophets in this sense? Not only those especially designated as such in the Old Testament, not only ordained ministers, but all believers. All true Christians are to be prophets of God, for the edification, exhortation of other believers and of unbelievers.[4]

Those who promote tongues, and seek to justify their emphasis Biblically, when referring to the Letter to the Corinthians only, and not to the Book of Acts, usually quote four verses of

1st Corinthians 14, namely: 4, 5, 18 and 39. Of these four verses, three of them are followed by a "but" or "yet" (verse 19 in connection with verse 18).

The remarkable thing now is that these points which Paul really directs against emphasis on the use of "glossolalia" are accepted for a proof by these people today. "I just speak mysteries in the Spirit, I only edify myself and this is commendable...."

We hear something like this again and again. One puts the emphasis on the opposite side of the little word, "but."

Yet this obviously contradicts the spirit and the basic principle of the teachings in chapter 14. It will not do to declare the counter-arguments of the apostle as positive points or even to recommend them.

With only just a little intellectual sincerity one ought to be able to recognize, and to learn, that the facts here are really twisted. The author of such an interpretation could not be the Holy Spirit, who will not, as we all well know, contradict His own Word.

This frequently-quoted verse four, "He that speaketh in an unknown tongue edifieth himself," giving this as a reason for speaking and praying in tongues, is completely reversing the intended meaning of the statement, as I understand it.

Strictly speaking, the apostle almost presents to the Corinthians an accusation or possibly a counter-argument. Gifts which are used for selfish purposes are highly questionable. Because the believers were puffed up (chapters four and five) it may not have been hard for them to live for their own edification and satisfaction, instead of the spiritual well-being of others.

John Stott, the well-known Anglican theologian, states:

"...While the tongue speaker "edifies himself" and therefore (Paul) is actively encouraging the practice of private tongue-speaking. I confess that I question whether this is the right deduction to draw. Two reasons make me hesitate.

First, "edification" in the New Testament is invariably a ministry which builds up others.

In addition, Christians have a ministry of "mutual upbuilding" (Romans 14:19) in which they are to "build one another up" (lst Thessalonians 5:11; Romans 15:2; Ephesians 4:29; Jude 20)

...Secondly we have to read the expression in the light of the teaching we have already considered, that all spiritual gifts are service gifts, bestowed "for the common good," for ministry to others...

So for these two reasons, it seems to me that there must be a note of irony, if not sarcasm, in Paul's voice as he writes of the tongue-speaker edifying himself.

He takes it for granted that the Corinthians, to whom he has clearly explained the purpose of spiritual gifts in chapter 12, will get his meaning and not need him to spell it out any further.[5]

Alfred Kuen considers this:

> One can even ask if the Apostle Paul, by the exceptional use of the verb (edifieth) in the reflexive form, does not want to draw the attention of the Corinthians, with a dash of irony, to a certain contradiction in phrases. Just as we would say of someone: "He loves himself and only serves himself," to distinguish between love and zealous service.[6]

Many a believer becomes intoxicated with a feeling of power which seems to be brought about by the possession of the Holy Spirit. Pastor Grant Swank makes a similar observation in *Christianity Today* about speakers-in-tongues who came into his church:

They were possessed with a counterfeit, a fake. They were living on an ego trip, a manufactured religious "high."[7]

Andrew Borland comes to similar conclusions:

The resurgence of interest in the gift has synchronized with the claim that it has been possible to have the "baptism of the Spirit" as an experience subsequent to conversion which enables some to exercise one or the other gifts mentioned in 1st Corinthians. That is an experience denied to the godliest of men of past and present generations, but claimed to be given to some whose conduct in the gatherings reveals emotional problems.[8]

William MacDonald writes in a similar way about 1st Corinthians 14:4:

This verse is usually given to justify the private use of tongues for self-edification. But the fact that we find the word "church" eight times in the same chapter (verses 4, 5, 12, 19, 23, 28, 34, 35) surely gives us the convicting proof that here Paul was not talking of an individual personal fellowship with God praying in our quiet little closet, but the use of tongues in the local church.

From this context one can see that here Paul does not recommend the speaking in tongues for self-edification at all but he condemns the use of this gift in the church as it does not help others.[9]

In any case, a spiritual person will seek the edification of the church and of others and not his own ecstacy (Romans 14:19). Let us again compare this with 1st Corinthians 10:24, 33. The carnal behavior of the Corinthians resulted in the alteration in the meaning of many things.

Michael Griffiths, also, does not seem to be very convinced of the private practice of this gift:

> What is implied by the words, "Let each of them keep silence in the church and speak to himself and to God" (14:28)? Does it mean that the use of tongues is a form of prayer which may equally be silent or spoken out loud? Or does it mean that the use of tongues should be confined to private devotions?
>
> It is this private use of tongues which is currently stressed in the Charismatic Movement. This is an argument from experience rather than Scripture. The actual Scriptural warrant for "solitary" speaking in tongues is not extensive. There is no example of it at all in the Acts narrative passages, and it is only understood by inference from the Corinthian passages.
>
> It could be urged; however, that in these chapters, Paul is dealing largely with the public use and not with the private exercise of this gift of tongues. Private use raises the additional problem that it is not susceptible to the Biblical test of genuineness in the way that public exercise may be. The individual is not able to apply these tests to himself when he is "inspired."[10]

A Bible teacher raised the question whether tongue speaking is intended for worship. Many charismatics claim to have a greater worship experience since they received the Spirit baptism. Now there are various gifts, talents and ministries.

But concerning worship and approaching God, all men are equal whether it is a simple cleaning woman or a gifted preacher, because God looks at the heart and He is not a respecter of persons.

Paul obviously expects an unequivocal "No" to the questions asked in 1st Corinthians 12:29–30: Are all apostles?

Are all prophets? Do all speak with tongues?). Thus, it is clear, God has not given this gift to every believer.

If a special form of worship were connected with this gift, then God would be the author of favoritism, in that He permits some of His children to worship Him better and thus have a deeper relationship than other believers. This would not be on the basis of the attitude of the Christian's heart, but rather because of an external gift.

But this is in conflict with the entire teaching of the Scriptures.

This results in divisions and party spirit, seen only too often in connection with the charismatic renewal.

Carriers of the gift of tongues often consider themselves to be more sanctified, to have received a little bit more of the Spirit, whilst others are sometimes declassified as "outer-court Christians." It fosters their pride.

These expositions make the so-called practicing of tongues for worship appear in a rather dubious light.

The remaining passage in 1st Corinthians 14 is a pretty obvious correction for the Corinthians for their practical use and promoting of tongues. Such an over-emphasis had to be rejected:

Verse 6:   "...what shall I profit you?"
Verse 7:   "...how shall it be piped and harped?"
Verse 8:   "...who shall prepare himself to battle?"
Verse 9:   "...for you shall speak in the air."
Verse 11:   "...Therefore if I know not the meaning of the
                   voice."
Verse 14:   "...my spirit prayeth, but my understanding is
                   unfruitful."

Concerning verses 14 and 15, I would like to quote from John Stott's book, *Your Mind Matters*:

Whatever Glossolalia may have been in New Testament days, whether a gift of foreign languages or of ecstatic utterance, the speech was certainly unintelligible to the speaker. And this is why Paul forbade its exercise in public if there was no one to translate or interpret, and discourage its exercise in private, if the speaker continued not to understand what he was saying.

He wrote: "Therefore he who speaks in a tongue should pray for the power to interpret. For if I pray in a tongue, my spirit prays but my mind is unfruitful. What am I to do? I will pray with the spirit and I will pray with the mind also" (1st Corinthians 14:13–15).

In other words, Paul could not contemplate any prayer or worship in which the mind was barren or inactive. He insisted that in all true worship, the mind must be fully and fruitfully engaged.

The Corinthians' cult of unintelligibility was a childish thing. They should indeed be as childish and innocent as possible in evil, but, he added, "in thinking be mature" (1st Corinthians 14:20).[11]

We read in verse 16: "…seeing he understandeth not what thou sayest." Verse 17: "…For thou verily givest thanks well, but the other is not edified." Verse 18 is often emphasized while verse 19 is generally overlooked — yet it is connected with verse 18.

Again the emphasis is on the "yet" and therefore on verse 19 and not on the oft-quoted verse 18, "Yet…I had rather speak five words with my understanding that I might teach others also, than ten thousand words in an unknown tongue."

The ratio was 1:2,000 and not vice versa. Now the question arises: May this ratio be taken so literally? The largest number in the Greek language was 10,000 — so today the contrast between these figures could also be rendered by 1:1 *million*.

John Stott writes in another passage of the above-mentioned book:

> Leaving aside questions regarding the validity of what they seek and claim, one of the most serious features at least of some Neo-Pentecostalism is its avowed anti-intellectualism.[12]

In closing, we can quote Spiros Zodhiates again:

> We have no record that this phenomenon occurred in any other New Testament church, nor did Paul ever seek to introduce it to them in the epistles. If it were the indispensable evidence of spirituality and the infilling of the Holy Spirit, we could certainly expect him to urge all believers to pray for this gift. Instead, he seeks to play it down among the Corinthians as much as possible.[13]

B. Tongues as a sign

Starting with verse 20, Paul introduces the Corinthians to a deeper level of understanding: "Brethren, be not children in understanding...but in understanding be men." Verse 22: "It is for a sign to them that believe not and not to them that believe."

The gift in Acts was a sign for the Jewish people, who had not yet accomplished a clear separation from the Old Covenant. Owing to signs given at this time, including the sign of tongues, they finally believed the whole Gospel of our Lord Jesus Christ.

In the 2nd chapter of the Book of Acts, we find how tongues were given as a sign to unbelievers. In one way, it was a reversal of the consequences of the Tower of Babel. In Genesis 11, God confused the languages, turned away from the nations and called an individual, namely Abraham (Genesis 12).

From then on, the revelations of God were only given to the Israelites in their own language. At Pentecost, God untangles the languages and this miracle indicated that now the counsel of God, the Gospel, becomes available to all people, "languages" and nations. Therewith the character of the new dispensation was revealed right at the beginning.

Just a note here: the tongues of today often show a disorderly Babylonish character, leading people to separate themselves. This rather indicates that the Lord, as in Genesis 11, is again turning away from the nations. The times of the gentiles are indeed coming to a close (Luke 21:24). The time is at hand when God will literally revive Israel out of its graves (Ezekiel 37).

According to 1st Corinthians 12:3, tongue-speaking is the use of a real language, not just babbling. The verse is often wrongly interpreted, as it is assumed that someone who maintains that Jesus is Lord must therefore have the Holy Spirit. This is contrary to Matthew 7:21–22 and other passages. The interpretation given to me by Evangelist Ralph Shallis of 1st Corinthians 12:2–3 explains it as follows:

First of all, the speaking in tongues must always be in a language, otherwise the interpreter would not know what was being said. When we find a phenomenon in the Bible for the first time, we also usually find the key to it. In Acts 2, it is clearly a question of languages as a miraculous sign. One is almost able to bring proof for this point of view from information science, that language means ORDER — [Greek: logos]; babbling means DISORDER — confusion; [Greek: alogos] — darkness.

The Holy Spirit is the Spirit of order (1st Corinthians 14:33), and the Lord Jesus Christ is called Logos (John 1:1). Secondly, this verse seems to indicate that, in ecstasy, one can also, instead of praising God, curse Christ.

Yet I would like to emphasize this: The people concerned very often do not have any consciousness of wrong and are sure that they are serving God and worshipping Him.

Their intentions are usually more than sincere. Sometimes they are like Peter who, in his zeal, wanted to keep Jesus from going to the cross and thought to serve God at the same time (Matthew 16:23).

However, in reality, Satan was the author (verse 23), and this in spite of the fact that just before (verse 16–17), the Spirit of God had clearly spoken through him. Although this happened before Pentecost, Peter's experience should awaken many to reality. The enemy knows how to manipulate fleshly zeal.

Very often it is found that the testing or questioning of the genuineness of the gifts is equated with the quenching of the Holy Spirit. It is claimed that we ought not to "judge." Yet the Holy Spirit does not contradict His Word (Revelation 2:2) and He commands us to prove everything (1st Thessalonians 5:21) even the spirits (1st John 4:1–3).

Concerning this area of deceit and testing Michael Griffiths writes:

> Because the gift is not self-authenticating, in 1st Corinthians 12:3 we are clearly warned to apply certain tests; it is therefore in accord with Scripture and not in any sense quenching the Spirit or tempting the Spirit to put the test of asking whether the spirit will confess that "Jesus is Lord."[14]

Again and again, we are told not to quench the Holy Spirit. This indeed should be avoided, yet to willfully change God's order and to turn it upside down, in my opinion, would quench the Holy Spirit much more. The least of the gifts, namely tongues, being exalted more and more today, shows us very clearly that something must be definitely wrong. Some churches even put their main emphasis on this gift. Here, obviously, the divine esteem and order has been replaced by another.

God is not a God of confusion (1st Corinthians 14:33). According to verse 37, the mark of a Spirit-filled life is not so much the emphasis of certain charismata, but rather the readiness to acknowledge the authority of the Word of God.

Why do more and more people believe that the gift of tongues indicates true spirituality and the fullness of the Spirit? Why do we meet more and more Christians today who cry to God for days and nights, animated by only one wish or desire, to finally receive this "beautiful" experience or charismata?

Today if we raise our voices in warning, we are accused of a lack of love. Love covers or tolerates, so it is claimed, these charismatic manifestations.

But do we not render ourselves guilty if we keep quiet in face of this distortion of divine standards? Of course, silence is a virtue, and in verse 34, women are commanded to keep silence. Because we will not acknowledge this, women are found in some circumstances to be leading more and more. Michael Griffiths observes in connection with verse 34:

> Nevertheless, this consideration may well give us reason to pause in view of the very considerable involvement of women in the "Glossolalia" movement.[15]

So the statement of one man of God must be repeated: "This movement does not stick to the Pauline rules." Only a soulish love will compromise and tolerate an unscriptural phenomena, gifts and error.

Real love, whereas it will accept the believer in Christ, will not contradict the Bible, but rejoices in the truth (1st Corinthians 13:6). Real love will also try to warn us, as Merrill F. Unger did in his book, *What Demons Can Do To Saints*.

> Prominent healers and charismatic leaders make a fatal blunder in mistaking these abilities for the genuine gifts of the

Spirit. They should renounce them. The ever-expanding charismatic confusion in the church today represents a clever halo-crowned stratagem of Satan to divide God's people and to bring them under a very subtle yet real type of occult bondage.[16]

Brethren who are under the influence of the false Pentecostal spirit are wrongly accusing discerning believers who question the current teachings regarding "gifts of the Spirit" and "tongues" by saying that they are defective in their understanding of the doctrine of the Holy Spirit.

Those brethren, in so doing, are really drawing a wrong battle line.

The fight is not directed against the gifts of the Spirit, or against mistakes and abuse of the charismata.

The struggle is against the false spirit, who imitates the divine gifts of grace and hides himself behind them, cunningly disguised. He would like to creep into the churches through these imitations and cause divisions by bringing "another gospel" while at the same time, casting a spell over the believers. It is very often a mixture of truth with error. Consequently, this spirit is more dangerous for the believers than open attacks and enmity.

I want to mention that the primary issue is not tongues and that they always are false or demonic. God may give them on special occasions. He is sovereign. But here this particular movement must be regarded as having a false source. There is enough potential in our flesh and emotions for such phenomena.

Finally, let us summarize: The initial use of tongues by the believers in Corinth was not an edifying gift. This letter proves that one can lead a carnal life marked by gross sins such as fornication, divisions, quarrels, et cetera, yet still be able to practice many charismata.

Gifts are not necessarily a criterion of spirituality and maturity. Many Corinthians were almost "specialists" in tongues, yet this gift presented a problem to the church. The believers are frankly labeled as carnal (1st Corinthians 3:1–3). The whole epistle had to be written due to a lack of church discipline at Corinth (chapter 5). Nearly everything was tolerated.

There is no shortcut to fullness of the Spirit. Holiness is not a sudden acquisition of spiritual maturity through an exciting experience, a way which our flesh would seem to prefer.

On the contrary, personal holiness is a process of growing through which we become more like our Lord Jesus, by the power of the Holy Spirit living in us and who gains room in our hearts on the basis of our obedience (Acts 5:32).

Point 3

LAYING ON OF HANDS

From personal experience, I wish to say that I was once open to the Charismatic Movement through David Wilkerson's book, *The Cross and the Switchblade*, and have been confronted with many false tongues in counselling.

Through the Charismatic Movement, we see an appalling infiltration of the churches and the believers.

Especially, the rapid laying on of hands has all too often had a disastrous result.

I do not generally disapprove of the laying on of hands, but the only case where we have a COMMAND concerning this practice in the New Testament, it is a warning and not an exhortation.

In 1st Timothy 5:22 we read: "Lay hands suddenly on no man." This is followed by the reason, "Neither be partaker of other men's sin: keep thyself pure." Although this may refer in particular to the ordination of elders, a general guideline may here be inferred.

As the laying on of hands implies an act of identification, perhaps we can understand why the Bible exhorts us to be cautious. As a result of painful experience, I have to say that carriers of false spirits lay on hands rapidly. The Holy Spirit is not transmitted through humans.

The Holy Spirit is God and "God that made the world and all things therein, seeing that he is Lord of heaven and Earth, dwelleth not in Temples made with hands; neither is worshipped with men's hands, as though he needed anything..." (Acts 17:24–25).

The Holy Spirit is given only by God, but in Pentecostalism, humans presume to dispense or even command God. By means of one's hand, one is ostensibly transmitting the Holy Spirit, and in my view, this also belongs to the fulfillment of 2nd Thessalonians 2:4: "...who exalts himself...." One is; in fact, unconsciously placing himself above God when he invites people thus: "Come up front, we will lay on hands, receive the

Spirit!" In other words, "We now have God at our disposal." This is ungodly.

Also, nowhere does the Bible command us to baptize people in the Spirit. It is said about the Lord Jesus that *He* is the baptizer, the function is not given to a human being or an especially "powerful" preacher.

The solemn fact is that a sudden laying on of hands or touching of any part of the body is the distinguishing mark of people involved in the occult, miracle healers, spiritists and spiritualists. Many believers have allowed themselves to be sucked into a similar trap.

It has long been observed that the carriers of such counterfeit spirits are urged inwardly, one can say almost controlled, to pass onto others this power which they have received themselves. This usually takes place through the laying on of hands or by the forming of a chain. One is driven to establishing physical contact.

Frank Holmes writes about true worship:

> There is no show, no display…It is not infectious. It is far removed from the group excitement engendered by the holding of hands and forming of circles common to witchcraft and other evil cults.[17]

One often feels a tingling or trembling sensation during the laying on of hands, or a flowing through of power, like an electric current or heat.

Such phenomena are not known in the Bible, but are very familiar in the realm of the occult, spiritism and psychic healing. Sometimes one gets dizzy, as when drunken, and even unconscious. We must remember that one of the fruits of the Holy Spirit is self-control.

In the widely-read book, *Nine o'clock in the Morning*, by Dennis Bennett, after the author had at last experienced the

"Spirit baptism," we read how his wife embraced and kissed him.

She told him that she already knew what had happened to him for she had known it the night before when something strange happened.

When he had come home, she was fast asleep, yet when he had opened the door, a current of power went through the house and woke her up.[18]

We are really faced with a very serious question here: What will become of our dear brothers in the Charismatic Movement if they confuse such obvious spiritism with the Holy Spirit? Moreover, what great danger will arise here for the church if such intermixture is no longer recognized and if such people continue to lay hands on others? It should be noted that Dennis Bennett ranks as a key figure or even "Father" of this whole Charismatic Movement.

A surgeon, who is an excellent counselor, was asked, "Doctor, what do you think of the Pentecostal and Charismatic Movement?" The doctor pointed to a large folder lying in front of him and said, "I have collected these documents which prove that each patient was worse after the laying on of hands." He probably did not mean the laying on of hands generally, but rather this overly-rapid Pentecostal, charismatic laying on of hands. Here, too, the incredible infiltration of the Temple of God is evident.

I have experienced cases where the sudden laying on of hands has resulted in incredible depression, compulsive thoughts or even suicide. How, then, has this surprisingly rapid infiltration become possible?

Now I believe that many dear Christians find it quite unthinkable that a reborn believer could receive a deceptive or false spirit. I thought so too for some time and although I had an inner inhibition, I asked a brother in the Lord, who was at that time a tongue-speaker, to lay hands on me.

After having read David Wilkerson's book, I also desired to receive the "Spirit baptism." My inner warning was brushed aside as I believed that we were both reborn and therefore nothing false could penetrate and affect me.

But is that really true? Is a genuine believer indeed beyond seduction and infiltration? Second Corinthians 11:4 strongly indicates that such an "invasion" seems possible but another proof is the Corinthian church itself.

Is Infiltration of a Believer Possible?

In the first 4 verses of 1st Corinthians, chapter ten, the Apostle Paul stresses the clear relationship of the Israelites to God.

They were the people of the living and true God. Verses 3 to 4 indicate that there were signs of real spiritual life. "And did all eat the same spiritual meat; and did all drink the same spiritual drink." If someone is eating and drinking he is undoubtedly alive.

In a similar sense, the Corinthians were genuine believers. Their sonship, or being part of Christ's body, was not questioned by the apostle.

Yet in relation to the Jews, Paul continues: "But with many of them God was not well pleased: for they were overthrown in the wilderness."

In the next verse, Paul relates this strongly emphasized warning to the Corinthian believers. In verses 7–10 one learns of a number of incidents where Israelites of the Old Covenant died under the judgement of God. Verse 11 declares that "these things happened unto them for ensamples; and they are written for our admonition."

There is no doubt that in his letters, Paul was giving counsel on actual spiritual problems which existed within the particular church to which he was writing. "Why," one might ask, "would the apostle mention these events? Why would he point out that so many died in this way?"

This aspect constituted a problem also for the Corinthians. There were people among them who, with God's permission, died physically. This is revealed in verse 30 of Chapter 11: "For this cause many are weak and sickly among you and many sleep." The expression, "sleep," means, in Greek, the same as having died.

In understanding this, the difficult verse 5 of chapter 5 can also be given a similar interpretation: "To deliver such an one unto Satan for the destruction of the flesh that the spirit may be saved in the Day of the Lord Jesus."

The person in question who committed this severe immorality should die as an expression of God's severe judgement (not one of eternal condemnation), even though he was a child of God, as the text specifically states, "…that the spirit may be saved." So, here we have an incredible intermixture. The old nature, because of gross sins, is in the grip of Satan; the new nature still belongs to Christ.

The possibility of this man repenting before he died cannot be discounted. Many commentators are convinced that the verses in 2nd Corinthians 2:5–11 referred; in fact, to this. If this is the case, then physical punishment would be withheld. These things have nothing to do with eternal life (1st Corinthians 11:32) but have a primary bearing on rewards (2nd John 7–8).

It is no coincidence that in chapter 3 of 1st Corinthians, the apostle deals with the subject of rewards. Such people are saved as by fire (1st Corinthians 3:15).

Now the question is, "When did God let His people (Old Covenant) and His children (New Covenant) die in judgement?" I deliberately formulate this question in the past tense, because I believe that at the beginning of every new era — as we shall point out later — God intervenes with signs. It is my conviction that, generally speaking, in the case of similar trans-gressions, the Lord no longer brings about such a physical pun-ishment.

Now, when did these Christians expose themselves to such a judgement of God? It is clear that one would not be stricken dead for some small transgression. As one considers the exam-ples above and other facts in Scripture, the conclusion is obvi-ous that God would let His people (Old Covenant) and His children (New Covenant) die in judgement if they were unre-pentant in the grip of Satan and in the fellowship of demons. If they, through severe iniquities, opened themselves to the adversary and were involved in the practice of grave sin, that would give an opportunity for the enemy of God to fill their hearts.

This was probably the case with Ananias and Sapphira (Acts 5: 1–5). Satan had filled Ananias heart (verse 3) and although a child of God, "he fell down and gave up the ghost" (verse 5). He had lied to the Holy Spirit (verse 3) which I believe can only be done by a believer. Since an unbeliever does not have the Holy Spirit (Romans 8:9), he cannot lie to Him.

The possibility of the intermingling of light and darkness, of the Holy Spirit and the spirit of Satan, of godliness and ungod-liness in one person, is actually strong meat. (See 1st Corinthians 3:2, Hebrews 5:13–14). Naturally such an inter-mixture does not exist in the invisible world, for the Holy Spirit never has fellowship with darkness. But man is a duality.

Paul is unable to discuss this directly with the carnal Corinthians, although he clearly tells them in an indirect way. In chapter ten, beginning in verse 14, he makes reference to the invisible spiritual mingling though idolatry in contrast to the visible mixing through fornication (carnal) referred to in chap-ter 6. God's answer to this, again, is "flee." In other words, one must completely and utterly separate oneself from anything that leads to fellowship with darkness.

In verses 16 – 20 of chapter ten, the apostle mentions the word "fellowship" or "Communion" three times and states very clearly in the second part of verse 20: "...and I would not, that ye should have fellowship with devils." This statement shows that it is possible for God's children to have fellowship with demons. One can only warn against something when it lies within the realm of possibility.

The following verses show that it is indeed possible, and, the extent to which the Corinthians were in fact already involved. "Ye cannot drink the cup of the Lord and the cup of devils; ye cannot be partakers of the Lord's table, and of the table of the devils. Do we provoke the Lord to jealousy? are we stronger than He?" (1st Corinthians 10:21–22).

The answer to this rhetorical question is, of course, "No." The proof of this was to be seen in the death of some believers in the church. God allowed them to die. He is the stronger One.

What Paul is endeavoring to say in these verses could be formulated thus: "You are in fellowship with demons. You drink of the cup of the Lord and also of the cup of demons." (In chapter 11, verse 20, he tells the Corinthians that it is not the Lord's Supper for which they come together).

"You are partakers of the table of demons. But this is an impossible situation, contrary to God, and your unrepentant behavior almost displays a defiance of God. One could almost believe you imagine yourselves to be stronger than God. But why do you have so many weak and sick and dead among you? Because it is God who is the stronger One which you can see among yourselves."

It is surely no coincidence that this letter brings out the principle of the transference of the powers of the invisible world from one person to another. This is the principle of identification, as pointed out before in relation with laying on of hands. Here we have another example: "What? know ye not that he which is joined to an harlot is one body? for two, says He, shall be one flesh. But he that is joined unto the Lord is one spirit" (1st Corinthians 6:16–17). In one instance, it is negative, in the other, positive.

Anyone who makes himself one with the Lord Jesus identifies himself with Him, which again is only possible at the cross. In doing so, he receives the Holy Spirit, and as he dies to self and grows in the Lord, may be filled more and more with the Spirit.

However, anyone joined to a harlot can receive unclean spirits and sins against his own body (verse 18). According to verse 19, the body is "the Temple of the Holy Ghost," and is in danger, through sins like these, of becoming the dwelling-place of Satan (2nd Corinthians 6:16a). This does not only mean the worst kind of intermixture, but even a fellowship of demons that is, of course, completely against God.

Such a person was in great danger of destroying the Temple of God and therefore of coming under the visible judgement of God, that is, physical death: "If any man defiles the Temple of God, him shall God destroy: for the Temple of God is holy, which Temple ye are" (1st Corinthians 3:17).

The stern warning of the apostle in chapter ten, verse eight, "Neither let us commit fornication, as some of them committed, and fell in one day three and twenty thousand," shows, without any doubt, the penalty to be physical death. Again, this verse in connection with 1st Corinthians 5:5 and 6:18 proves that in judgement, God can destroy our Temple and allow us to die. The above verses stand for carnal fornication, 1st Corinthians 10:7 and 10:20–22 for spiritual fornication; that was idolatry also resulting in death (11:29–30) at the time of the early church.

The apostle does not mention this by chance, as these were precisely the two main problems of intermixture prevalent in that church. It reminds one of the doctrine of Balaam, "who taught...to eat things sacrificed unto idols, and to commit fornication" (Revelation 2:14).

It is possible for a believer to unite himself visibly with another person in an ungodly relationship through fornication and adultery. Similarly, this is also possible in the invisible world. As believers we know that these seducing spirits are personal beings. These two aspects of intermixture usually run parallel. Thus we read in Revelation 2:20, "Notwithstanding I have a few things against thee, because thou sufferest that woman Jezebel, which calleth herself a prophetess, to teach and to seduce my servants to commit fornication, and to eat things sacrificed to idols." And physical punishment is predicted here too: "And I will kill her children with death" (verse 23).

It is this mixture taking place in the seen and unseen world that the Corinthian situation was all about. They were literally permeated with leaven and therefore exhorted to purge it out (1st Corinthians 5:7). On the one side, they had the carnal relationship with darkness, and on the other side, they were indwelt by the Holy Spirit.

Because of an infiltration by deceiving spirits, the Corinthians were eagerly yearning for sensational gifts, and especially those of tongues. Paul, as we have shown before, opposes this perilous emphasis.

The situation as we see it today shows a strong parallel with the Corinthian church. The Corinthians were limited in their growth (children), immoral in their way of life, tolerated evil, were charismatic in their practices, and heretical in their teachings. George Gardiner writes:

> But not only was the city tragically like our civilization, the
> church of Corinth was tragically like a large segment of
> Christendom in our days…It has been said that the letters to
> the Corinthians are the most relevant books of the New
> Testament for the last half of the twentieth century. Truer
> words were never spoken.[19]

As already mentioned, this intermixture is strong meat. Had the
apostle told the carnal Corinthians this directly, it would have
been too much for them due to their spiritual immaturity. It is
a fact that many immature believers become confused and
upset when speaking about this subject. They either refuse to
consider the matter or continually torment themselves with the
(false) thought that perhaps he too can be "possessed." Both
reactions are wrong.

In his second letter to the Corinthians, the Apostle Paul
informed them of this directly, for they had become more
mature and had partly repented. In the already mentioned passage of 2nd Corinthians 11:4, we read the not-very-flattering
words: "…or if ye receive another spirit…ye might well bear
with him…."

Another reason for such infiltration lies in the phenomenon
of passivity. I would like to discuss it in greater detail.

Point 4

PASSIVITY

It was really the secular researchers who made passivity clear to me in a completely new way. Here, I am talking particularly about the two world-famous brain researchers, Sir John Eccles and Wilder Penfield. Perhaps the most famous is Sir John Eccles, who is a Nobel Prize winner.

A. The Identity Theory
These scientists discovered (on the basis of their brain research) that the "Identity Theory" of the materialists is false.

What do we mean by "Identity Theory"? When explaining to a materialist that man consists of more than the visible, that he has an invisible identity, that is, an immortal soul, he will probably answer that this is all pious nonsense. He does not believe it exists. He says my personality, my so-called soul, is only the sum of highly complicated electrochemical sequences in my brain. When my brain stops, my personality also stops.

Sir John Eccles and Wilder Penfield realized that this "Identity Theory" is incorrect. They discovered that our brain is comparable to a complicated machine which is utilized by an invisible being which Eccles called the "self." From this, we see that, in reality, the brain itself cannot think at all!

What really "thinks" is a spirit which utilizes the brain from a superior position. These secular scientists compared the brain to a piano, and we can see that it is not the *piano* that is ultimately important, but rather the *player*.

These researchers also realized that it is not exclusively a person's spirit which can operate the brain, but that other spirits or a spirit in general can also do this. Our "self" thinks with the brain, just as the data processor operates a computer.

With this fact, that our brain is a machine which does not think by itself but instead is used, the phenomenon of compulsive and blasphemous thoughts is connected.

The receiving of thoughts, pictures and visions against one's will is becoming an increasingly prevalent phenomenon.

Many believers also suffer from these compulsions and this is usually connected with the existence of occult claims through which the foreign spirit can still switch himself into this highly complicated mechanism of the brain.

Converts from the drug scene, for example, sometimes still suffer from flashbacks for a time after their conversion. Through a life of sanctification, such things are usually eliminated.

I have heard several testimonies of former hippies, drug addicts and others who have told me of these experiences. This reminds one of 2nd Corinthians 7:1: "...let us cleanse ourselves from all filthiness of the flesh and spirit, perfecting holiness in the fear of God." Here Paul talks about defilement among believers, which is removed through a life of holiness.

Paul mentions defilement of flesh and spirit. As I understand it, defilement of flesh means sexual sins and defilement of spirit refers to the occult or idolatrous transgressions.

This was, at least in part, the situation in Corinth. Paul exhorts us to flee fornication (1st Corinthians 6:18), and to flee idolatry (1st Corinthians 10:14).

Today, we have, at least in the Western World, a wave of sex and the occult. Because of that we can see more and more situations like that in the church of Corinth, with special emphasis on tongues and supernatural gifts.

People who are defiled in flesh or spirit tend to demonstrate exactly this ungodly mixture Paul is listing previous to 2nd Corinthians 7:1, namely chapter six, verse 14: "Be ye not unequally yoked together with unbelievers: for what fellowship hath righteousness with unrighteousness? And what Communion hath light with darkness?" In 2nd Corinthians 6:13, Paul exhorts the believers to be enlarged and to be filled with Christ and His Word, and then to restrict association with the world (verse 14) and come out from amongst them (verse 17). On the other hand, we should be balanced.

Now, the Ecumenical and Charismatic Movements literally yoke together light and darkness, believers and unbelievers, church and world. As, according to the development of these last days, the defilement of flesh and spirit amongst believers increases, parallel with it runs the sympathy for the Charismatic and Ecumenical Movement.

Dave Hunt wrote in *The Psychic War*, an unpublished manuscript,

"The Nobel Prize winner and world-famous brain researcher Sir John Eccles once described the human brain as a machine which can be operated by a spirit. Normally my personality is the spirit which operates my brain. But if I enter an altered state of consciousness and relinquish control to a power, which a spiritualist or meditation teacher calls a cosmic strength or a medium describes as a spirit, then nothing prevents this new spirit from running my brain and producing experiences which may appear very real to me but do not occur in reality."

B. Active or Passive?

In general, it must be said that following Christ and praying are always active. The Bible says, "strive, seek, ask, knock, chase after, resist, test, flee" et cetera. Paul writes to the Colossians, "For I would that ye knew what great conflict I have for you" (Colossians 2:11). We are instructed to be watchful and this is the very opposite of passivity.

Please do not misunderstand me. We are called to have a "quiet time" and to be silent before the Lord, but this is never with a passive mind. May I remind you of Joshua 1:7–8 or Psalm 1, where we are exhorted to feed on the Word and meditate upon, or think about, and memorize it.

This is the way to fruitful service and discipleship and is the very opposite of a passive mind. I would like to place these fundamental facts in juxtaposition. The Holy Spirit causes self-control. The false spirit seeks direct control. Galatians 5:23 quotes the Greek word "enkrateia" — which also means self-control — as one of the fruits of the Holy Spirit.

The Holy Spirit illuminates the understanding, while the false spirit switches it off. The Holy Spirit, the Spirit of truth, makes one watchful and active. The false spirit, the spirit of error, makes one passive. The Spirit of truth influences my heart; the spirit of error uses my body. The Holy Spirit enables my "self" (in Biblical anthropology, my soul, Greek "psyche") to operate this machine with an increasing efficiency.

The concept of my "self," my personality, is best explained from the story in Luke 16 about the rich man and poor Lazarus. When this rich man is dead and in Hades, he is there as a complete person, although his body and his brain are decomposed and dead. He talks, he has feelings, he recognizes Lazarus, et cetera. That which is still completely present is the personality of the rich man, which we may call his "psyche."

The Holy Spirit enables me to utilize this machinery increasingly well, but He will never interfere directly, because God respects the order of His creation and loves His creatures. He has restricted Himself here and does not manipulate man. Therefore the Bible declares: "and the spirits of the prophets are subject to the prophets" (1st Corinthians 14:32).

I would like to give an appalling example for this phenomenon of passiveness. The ability to piously camouflage is well illustrated in a book published by one of the biggest spiritist lodges of Europe, namely the "Spiritualist Lodge" in Zurich. The book is called *Contact with the Spirit World* and under the title "Education of Mediums," the following is quoted in answer to the question, "How does one become a medium?"

> He starts with a short prayer, has a short reading from the
> Holy Scriptures and thinks about that which he has read.

This sounds very pious and absolutely Biblical. But how does it continue?

> Then, as instructed before, he holds his hand with a pencil on a piece of paper lying in front of him and waits without any mental tension. If he is motivated to write down thoughts which are inspired in him with great definiteness, he should write them down. If his hand is moved by a foreign force, he should yield.[20]

Or think about the comment made by a missionary who is often in India, "If you go to a soothsayer in India, the first thing she will say is 'Make your mind a blank, let yourself fall, open yourself!'"

The Bible says "resist!" We should also consider that every hypnotist works on the basis of passivity. The condition of his successful hypnosis is that people open themselves to him. He will frankly admit that he cannot do anything if someone is not willing to follow him or resists him.

Here the Bible warns us clearly to be watchful and resist. Following the example I have mentioned above, I want to stress that one finds the very same practice of passivity among the adherents of the Pentecostal and Charismatic Movement.

In stating this we do not mean that these people are not real Christians.

A born-again believer can also be infiltrated by a false spirit as we read in 2nd Corinthians 11:4, "For if he that cometh preacheth another Jesus, whom we have not preached, or if ye receive another spirit, which ye have not received, or another gospel, which ye have not accepted, ye might well bear with him."

It is just here that we find the greatest ignorance and lack of awareness, as many dear Christians cannot conceive that such a mixture is possible.

Reverend David Gardiner, author of *The Trumpet Sounds for Britain*, puts it in a very concise way when he writes:

> I have come to the conclusion that there must be also another spirit at work in the Charismatic Movement which is definitely not the Spirit of Jesus, even if the Holy Spirit is also at work.[21]

The general situations outlined above do not mean that no good people are ever to be found in these movements, for it has to be admitted that honest and upright Christians are involved in it. But we must understand that a child of God can also make himself passive.

The Apostle Peter does not mean unbelievers, but rather real Christians when he says, "Be sober, be vigilant; because your adversary the devil, as a roaring lion, walketh about, seeking whom he may devour: whom resist..." (1st Peter 5:8–9).

People with drug or occult backgrounds are inclined to passivity and this explains why converts out of this environment are so prone to the Charismatic Movement.

C. Passivity Among These Modern Movements

Completely disregarding the Biblical teaching about man's personality, the charismatic or Pentecostal circles proclaim the Holy Spirit's direct use of the human body and mind, such as speaking out of him as if he were a spiritist medium.

Conscious of generalization, I want us to note that all movements of this kind — be it the Pentecostal Movement of Los Angeles 1906, the Charismatic Movement with its beginning about 1960 or the Catholic Charismatic Movement which began in 1967 — in every case these groups began with prophecies introduced by these words: "Thus says the Lord." However, we do not find this formulation anywhere in the New Testament, because it is limited solely to the Old Testament.

We must keep in mind that the New Testament inspiration works in a different manner. At the beginning of the letters by Paul or Peter — which are unquestionably the Word of God — we do not see the statement, "Thus says the Lord." We can perceive, for example, Paul's particular style of writing, his personal wishes, et cetera.

Here, we can clearly state that the whole human personality of the individual writer is used by God. Even admitting the fact that the inspiration will remain a mystery which cannot be completely comprehended, we must maintain that the Holy Spirit never eliminates the human mind and personality. Rather, we observe a wonderful harmony between the Holy Spirit and the human personality. Nowhere in Scripture do we find an elimination of the latter.

As the direct speaking of the Holy Spirit through human beings is believed in pseudo-charismatic circles (as these movements really should be called), this will explain the occasional strong feeling of self-importance which often results in pride and stubbornness against strong doctrine.

If anyone doubts the origin and Biblical basis of these prophecies or even "I, Jesus" messages, the doubter will often be accused of having blasphemed the Holy Spirit.

Any uncertainty as to whether the Spirit has directly spoken is considered wrong. The Biblical attitude of alertness is even taken as sin against the Holy Spirit.

Again, these erroneous views arise from a completely wrong understanding of the Biblical teaching of the Holy Spirit (pneumatology) and of human personality (anthropology).

If God really speaks more or less normally today through such prophecies or visions or dreams, then this becomes the *present* Word of God and the Bible becomes the *past* Word. Why then bother to feed upon the Word? This reveals the true interest of the enemy, for man "shall not live by bread alone, but by every word that proceedeth out of the mouth of God"

(Matthew 4:6). This is one of the most subtle attacks, in Biblical disguise, against the authority of the Holy Scriptures.

Followers of this movement, that is, speakers-in-tongues, believe according to this understanding, by usually quoting verses of 1st Corinthians 14, insisting that the Holy Spirit speaks or prays directly through or in them.

But the word "Holy Spirit" is never mentioned in 1st Corinthians 14.

Spiros Zodhiates writes:

> We also note that the term: "Holy Spirit" does not occur at all in connection with speaking with tongues in 1st Corinthians 14. Whenever the words "spirit" or "spirits" occur in this chapter, they always refer to man's spirit.[22]

We can therefore conclude that when Paul states in 1st Corinthians 14:14, "For if I pray in an unknown tongue, my spirit prayeth..." and in 1st Corinthians 14:32: "...the spirits of the prophets are subject to the prophets" — this clearly refers to the human spirit.

A comparison will make clear that the charismatic practice — due to the conviction that the Holy Spirit would be praying in and through them — has to be categorized as mediumistic. Arnold Bittlinger, who could be called the father of the Charismatic Movement in Germany, writes in his book, *Glossolalia*:

> Many Christians have experienced that "it" is constantly praying in them — even when they are silent or their thoughts are occupied with work.[23]

These are typical symptoms and phenomena of a false spirit, not the Spirit of truth but the spirit of error. Contrary to this, the Holy Spirit works it out that I pray and that I speak. He will not do that for me, because God never encourages laziness or passiveness.

Perhaps we now understand why, in the teaching about His Second Coming, the Lord Jesus so often repeats Himself concerning vigilance and watchfulness.

Today, yoga, autogenic training, transcendental meditation, drugs, the Charismatic Movement, much from TV, the hard beat and rock music and so-on, thrive on passivity. You let yourself fall, you drift away, you make your mind blank, and consequently, you open yourself up and surrender yourself to an evil power. Against that, we hear the warning voice of Scripture: Be watchful!

The above-mentioned quotation by Arnold Bittlinger became very real to me while counselling a young man entangled in autogenic training and who later became converted. He described his basic teaching from autogenic training as expressed in the sentence, "I am breathed" or "it breathes me."

Depending on the intensity of the influence of darkness and counterfeit spirits, I am really distressed to say that often people are not only partly, but sometimes fully temporarily controlled by evil spirits. This results in being thrown to the floor, "slain in the spirit," fainting, et cetera (See 1st Corinthians 12:2).

Here we read: "Ye know that ye were gentiles, carried away unto these dumb idols, even as ye were led." The Menge (German) Bible renders it, "...being snatched away." The Greek word, "apagomenoi" is the passive participle of "apago." This passive form (apagomai) reads literally: "to be torn or pulled away."

It is also worth mentioning that this verse points out how the idols are dumb (aphonos). In paganism, the communication does not go by the mind (nous), but by emotions and ecstasy. The more someone is beside himself, the closer he is to his deity, which all too often is perceived like a physical force (energy, heat, electric current, and so-forth). The whole line of argument by Paul in 1st Corinthians 14, in the verses 6 to 19, is to show how that which is uttered must be understood. Otherwise, it feeds the irrationality and has more parallels to paganism than Christianity.

Back to the previous thought: If someone is led away against his will, then this is done through a false spirit, because the fruit of the Spirit is self-control. The Apostle Paul, in effect, says to the Corinthians: "Well, you know; while you were still gentiles, it just drew you to these dumb idols. Like robots you were pulled away."

If things like these are happening again today, it is hard to understand why all of a sudden it should be considered to be produced by the Holy Spirit.

This is even more noteworthy, as the apostle explains in that verse how to discern the false gifts and their manifestations.

Watchman Nee writes:

> The satanic spirit; however, so puts the person under the oppression of an external power that it appears to him to represent God's will and compels him to act like a machine devoid of thought or decision.[24]

In this context, the following report from the books of Kathryn Kuhlman is highly informative and instructive:

> And I fell to the floor. Later Donna told me that while I had been lying on the floor, I had banged my left leg up and down with such force that she had been afraid it would break. After a while, some ushers helped me on to my feet again and escorted me to the platform.[25]

Let us imagine this for a moment: A person is lying helplessly on the floor with a quivering leg, furiously kicking it up and

down. This reminds us, objectively speaking, rather of possession, a temporary seizure by an alien force, than of the work
of God.

"Be self-controlled and alert," renders the NIV of 1st Peter
5:8.

The Lord or the apostles never had meetings where people
were "slain in th Spirit" and fell over backwards while atten-
dants were handily positioned to catch them.

At this point I do not wish to attack any person, but I would
like to warn against the powers which hide themselves behind
such manifestations.

In the meetings of Reinhard Bonnke, the famous German
Pentecostal preacher in the south of Africa, those who come
forward are slain to the ground:

> When Pastor Bonnke laid his hands on me, a stream of God's
> power went through my body and I collapsed to the floor
> under the power. While I lay on the floor, I was in the spirit
> with Jesus in heaven.

Or,

> The crowd is gathered for the baptism in the Holy Spirit.
> Five seconds later, all 3500 were slain to the ground under
> the power of God, speaking in new tongues. This was the
> greatest scene of its kind in the history of South Africa.[26]

Another appalling example is Benny Hinn. It is interesting to
learn about the source of his "anointing."

> In an April 7, 1991 sermon, Hinn revealed that he periodi-
> cally visits [Kathryn] Kuhlman's grave and that he is one of
> the few with a key to gain access to it. He also visits Aimee's
> [McPherson, founder of the Foursquare Gospel church]

> grave, were he says: "I felt a terrific anointing...I was shaking all over...trembling under the power of God.... 'Dear God,' I said, 'I feel the anointing.'...I believe the anointing has lingered over Aimee's body."
>
> The anointing power plays a major role at Benny Hinn's "miracle services." He uses it to "slay in the spirit" as Kuhlman did 30 years ago. She has been imitated by charismatic evangelist/healers ever since. But Hinn has a new flare. Yes, like Kuhlman, he touches people on the forehead or neck to make them fall over. But he also blows or throws the "anointing" and "slays" people from a distance....
>
> As a catcher moves to pick up a woman, Hinn slays him...then he slays the catcher who caught the catcher.... He blows loudly in the microphone....Hundreds fall backward... a woman collapses in the aisle and begins to babble. And then, suddenly, Benny is gone. The power vanishes from the room, and the people stare in stunned silence.[27]

This evil power also uses the material world to achieve results. Therefore we observe, as already mentioned, the arbitrary or rapid laying on of hands, because physical contact is often necessary to transfer the false spirit. "The Charismatics have a magic concept of God," a famous Anglican theologian told me in a private conversation.

Kenneth Hagin, for example, who proclaims a message of health and prosperity through positive faith declares:

> I lay hands on you by direction of the Head of the church, Jesus Christ, and in obedience to the Law of Contact and Transmission. The contact of my hands transmits God's healing power...There it is! There it is!..."[28]

Depending on the intensity of infiltration, these evil powers will gradually gain control of the human brain, soon being able to operate or manipulate it like a machine. As a result, we see an increasing number of reports of people hearing voices, having dreams, visions, appearances of angels and so on. Some even claim to have seen Jesus. Again I must call this the work of a counterfeit spirit, following mediumistic principles.

While saying this, I do not mean that each supernatural dream or each miraculous event (I do believe in divine healing, especially according to James 5) must be false or demonic.

I do wish to point out; however, that today's increasing incidence of supernatural phenomena, particularly healings, as predicted for the last days, have a false power as a driving force.

Another example of this is Demos Shakarian, the founder of the Full Gospel Business Men's Fellowship International, abbreviated FGBMFI, a movement which has greatly stimulated the Charismatic Movement. Upon receiving his baptism of the Spirit, he sensed an invisible power pulling him to the floor. One can read in his book, *The Happiest People on Earth*, where he describes his experience as follows:

> I sank to the floor and lay there on the rug absolutely helpless, unable to get up and get into bed.[29]

Conversely, the Holy Spirit always brings about self-control into our lives. Here is a man who obviously had lost self-control. This grave, serious term, "demon possession," means that someone else is in possession of me so that I am not able to do what I want to do. I lose control of my brain or part of my body.

Similar phenomena, where people lose self-control and allow themselves to be controlled, take place at meetings with John Wimber. He reports about the history of his work in a message given in 1980 at Yorba Linda:

> The Holy Spirit fell on us...I walked up to a woman to pray
> for her and I raised my hand and she went flying...Bam!
> Against the wall she went, over a couch, knocked over a
> table and a lamp and hit the corner. Now she had a bad neck
> she wanted to be prayed for...
>
> Another guy fell against me and hit me in the chest speak-
> ing in tongues like a machine gun...I thought, "What have
> we released here? This is weird!" The moment they touched
> me, we both went down and there was the sense, the pres-
> ence of something in the room. God!
>
> ...I went home and I was sort of drunken...I said to Carol
> [his wife] "I think we are in for something," and when I said
> that, I went right to the floor!... One girl fell so hard,
> I thought, "Oh no, she is gonna die. She hit her head on a
> chair and on a table and on the floor. Bam! bam! bam!..."
>
> Then I heard about catchers. So we got a catcher.[30]

Again we recognize the classical symptoms of mediumistic
powers. We sadly meet this throughout the whole Charismatic
Movement. Even the very outset, the so-called baptism of the
Spirit of Agnes Ozman, who according to Pentecostal history
was the first person in our century to speak in tongues, betrays
already this lack of self-control.

Charles Parham, founder of the Pentecostal Movement, who
was later on arrested for the the grossest of immoralities,
recalled:

> I laid my hands upon her [Agnes Ozman] and prayed. I had
> scarcely repeated three dozen sentences when a glory fell
> upon her, a halo seemed to surround her head and face, and
> she began speaking in the Chinese language and was unable
> to speak English for three days. When she tried to write in
> English to tell us of her experience, she wrote Chinese....[31]

These handwritings turned out to be no language at all, but just unintelligible scribbling.

Referring to Ephesians 5:18 John Stott writes the following:

> The Greek word "asotia"…literally describes a condition in which a person cannot "save" or control himself. It is because drunkenness involves a loss of self-control, Paul writes, that it should be avoided. It is implied that the contrasting state, the fullness of the Spirit, involves no loss of self-control. On the contrast, we are distinctly told in Galatians 5:23 that a part of the fruit of the Spirit is self-control (enkrateia)![32]

In this context, it should be interesting to note what G.H. Lang writes in his book, *The Earlier Years of the Modern Tongues Movement*, going back to the beginning of the Pentecostal Movement, in Los Angeles in 1906:

> A woman rose in a meeting and moved toward the piano. Her husband, knowing she could not play, shut the piano to avoid fiasco. But she, though walking among the seats with her eyes tightly closed, reaches the piano safely, opened it and played musically.[33]

This is a classic example of the working of counterfeit spirits. The "biological machine" of the woman served as a tool for the seductive spirit which played the piano through her. In this sense, she only acted as a medium.

The testimony of T.B. Barratt, who is called the father of European Pentecostalism, is very similar. He describes his own baptism of the Spirit, which he received on November 5, 1906 as follows:

> The power came so suddenly, that I lay on the floor speaking
> in tongues incessantly for some time. In fact, I kept on,
> mostly speaking in tongues...it seemed as if an iron hand
> laid over my jaws. Both jaws and tongues were worked by
> this unseen power.[34]

Here too, we notice the characteristic symptoms of mediumism. Also, nowhere in the epistles do the apostles urge the believers to seek a second experience of baptism of the Spirit as Barratt did.

In a German Pentecostal magazine, Paul Yonggi Cho, pastor of the world's largest church in Seoul, South Korea, relates his conversion and subsequent healing from tuberculosis. After stating how Jesus stood beside him wearing a crown of thorns with blood running down His Temples, he continues:

> My tongue and my lips began to speak. I tried to stop, but it
> appeared as if another person controlled my tongue and
> wanted to express himself forcefully. I did not know what it
> was, but I realized the more I spoke, the better I felt.[35]

The evil spirits very often attack the nervous system of their victims. Many who have spoken in tongues, after seemingly having experienced wonderful "blessings," end up with nervous breakdowns, uncontrolled emotionalism, or worse in psychiatric hospitals, or even gross immorality. The evangelist R. A. Torrey warned:

> The "Tongues Movement" has been accompanied by the
> most grievous disorders and the grossest immoralities...In a
> number of instances men and women leaders in the move-
> ment have proven guilty of the vilest relations to one another.
> In many instances, the movement has seethed with immoral-
> ity of the grossest character.

This is not to say for a moment that there are no clean-minded and well-meaning men and women in the movement, but the movement as a whole has apparently developed more immorality than any other modern movement except spiritism, to which it is so closely allied in many ways.[36]

D. Falling on One's Back

Perhaps it is also noteworthy that in such healing meetings, participants often fall physically onto their backs. This was the case with Kathryn Kuhlman, in the campaigns of Reinhard Bonnke, at some meetings of John Wimber and of YWAM, as reported to me in Germany, and at some chapter meetings of the FGBMFI and, of course, also at various other gatherings. The phenomenon of being "slain in the Spirit" is explained as a work of God. One of the latest developments is labeled the "Toronto Blessing."

When Reinhard Bonnke laid hands on me, I was thrown backward falling onto a stone floor, as if had been struck by lightning and I lost all sense of feeling. Each physical sensation left me. I was not hurt by this sudden fall.[37]

I would like to make it very clear that the Holy Spirit never acts in this way. In the presence of God, if a person falls at all, he would fall on his face, (1st Kings 18:39, Matthew 17:6, Luke 17:16 among others) which is a sign of submission.

First Corinthians 14:25 is quite explicit — this being the favorite chapter of adherents to the Charismatic Movement — that the man convicted by the Holy Spirit will fall down on his face.

Are there any Biblical references to falling on one's back? The passages which mention this phenomenon are clearly referring to the judgement of God. When the high priest Eli heard that the Ark of the Covenant was stolen by the

Philistines, he fell backwards off his stool and died (1st Samuel 4:18). God had declared that He would bring judgement upon his house (1st Samuel 2:34).

An allegoric passage indicating similar aspects might be Genesis 49:17.

In Isaiah 28:7, God speaks of the judgment upon the false prophets. Finally, verse 13 says: "...that they might go and fall backwards, and be broken, and snared and taken." Very often this being "slain in the Spirit" is accompanied by speaking in tongues.

This reminds one of the passage in Isaiah 29:4, "And thou shalt be brought down, and shalt speak out of the ground, and thy speech shall be low out of the dust, and thy voice shall be, as of one that hath a familiar spirit, out of the ground, and thy speech shall whisper out of the dust."

Falling upon one's back indicates the uncovering of one's nakedness before God. For this reason the altar in the Old Testament times could not be built upon steps: "Neither shalt thou go up by steps unto mine altar, that thy nakedness be not discovered thereon" (Exodus 20:26).

The man who falls upon his face hides his nakedness before a holy God. It is the spirit of the enemy of God that uncovers man (Revelation 16:15). This phenomenon is a classical example of either demonic influence or a demonstration of God's judgement.

E. Out-of-body Experience

Depending on how strong the claims of evil powers may be upon my soul, these forces can even remove my inner self or my invisible being out of my body. This is called out-of-body experience (OBE) and a known phenomenon of high grade spiritism.

In the same category belong the death experience, detailed in Kuebler-Ross' reports and Raymond Moody's bestseller,

Life after Life, in which people gave the account of having the feeling of being outside their own body, sitting or lying somewhere in the distance.

I mention this, because you find it more and more in Christian literature. Again, for example, Demos Shakarian, in his above mentioned book, *The Happiest People on Earth*, describes the vision which resulted in the founding of the FGBMFI. Here, Demos Shakarian experiences himself suspended over the Earth.

At the end of his visions, he returns to his home in Downey, California, in which he sees himself kneeling in prayer. This is an excursion of the soul, OBE, dressed in religious apparel.

Another book which is widely circulated is Bilquis Sheik's *I Dared to Call Him Father*. This is the conversion story of a Muslim lady from Pakistan who also experienced an excursion of the soul.

A further book is Roland Buck's *Angels on Assignment*, where such phenomena are reported.

Kenneth Hagin, a key leader of the so-called "Faith Movement," has had several OBE's. Not only does Hagin boast about alleged visits to heaven and hell, but in his writings, he recounts numerous out-of-body experiences (OBE's) in vivid detail. During his conversion in 1933, Hagin reports he had a near-death, out-of-body experience:

> I slipped back into my body as a man slips into his trousers
> in the morning, the same way in which I had gone out —
> through my mouth.[38]

It is frightening to see how these phenomena are spreading. How necessary it is for us to be watchful in our days.

Point 5

SIGNS AND WONDERS

Again and again, we hear in our days of an increasing emphasis on signs and wonders. John Wimber from California, for example, has coined a new phrase called "Power Evangelism." He is certain that only accompanying signs and miracles will convince unbelievers on a large scale of the truth of the Gospel.

So here we want to search the Scriptures and deal with this aspect. Are signs and wonders a promise for each "spirit-filled" preacher and evangelist, or were they mainly confined to the apostolic age?

In the following passage, I have taken many ideas from John Whitcomb's brilliant article, *Modern Science and Biblical Miracles*.

SIGNS IN THE GOSPEL OF JOHN

Very often, believers seek for a visible, tangible proof that the Word of God is true and reliable.

Would it not strengthen our faith, for example, to be in Palestine and actually see Jesus perform those miracles before our very eyes? Would this not make us mature and confirm our faith immediately?

Yet, this is a totally false approach. In fact, one purpose of the Gospel of John is to demonstrate that no one can really be converted by observing miracles. Nor can anyone become truly mature in the Christian faith by that empirical method.

Why? Let us, for example, examine John 2:23: "Now when he (Jesus) was in Jerusalem at the passover...many believed in his name, when they saw the miracles which he did."

Now, you could say, "Here it is, here are people who believed in Christ because they saw His miracles. Many followed Jesus because they saw the signs. If we also could perform signs and wonders, many would believe."

However, notice the next two verses: "But Jesus did not commit himself unto them, because he knew all men, and needed not that any should testify of man: for he knew what was in man."

This kind of faith was not of such a sort that could enable the Lord to commit Himself to those people. He knew the hearts of these followers and that their beliefs were only superficial, based on sense experience.

A. The Case of Nicodemus

Now, this is explained in the following chapter of John's Gospel, and we have to read the whole passage in its context. Attention is focused on one of this kind of "believers," namely Nicodemus. "The same came to Jesus by night, and said unto him, Rabbi, we know that thou art a teacher come from God: for no man can do these miracles that thou doest, except God be with him" (John 3:2).

Undoubtedly, Nicodemus believed in the miracles of Jesus. So one would think that the Lord might be thrilled to hear such a testimony from a man of this stature. Wouldn't he give a new impetus to this new movement which till then consisted mainly of fishermen and a tax collector?

Now, we know that this is exactly what the Lord did *not* say. The Lord replied with the famous statement: "Verily, verily I say unto thee, Except a man be born again, he cannot see the kingdom of God" (John 3:3).

In other words: "Nicodemus, you are so far from the kingdom that you can't even see it. You have seen signs and miracles, yet you are spiritually dead. You must be born again."

Why? Didn't he believe in the miracles?

Of course he did.

But here, from this Gospel, we can learn that belief in what your senses tell you does not save a person.

The true belief is on a much higher level and Nicodemus did not have this belief. Yet, it is this belief you and I must have in order to have eternal life.

We have to realize that we are lost sinners and under the judgement of God. We must understand that only faith in His Son can save us from the future wrath and that we are by nature utterly corrupt and must be born again.

And as this famous chapter points out so clearly, we are not born again by observing signs and wonders, but by real faith in the Lord Jesus and His atoning work upon the cross and His word. "Verily, verily, I say unto you, He that heareth my word, and believeth on him that sent me, hath everlasting life" (John 5:24).

But seeing miracles is by no means a guarantee of salvation or eternal life. There is a heaven or hell distinction between accepting empirical evidence through your sense experiences at face value and, on the other hand, recognizing God's eternal truth concerning Himself and man in a spiritual state of judgement. We must understand the truths of the finished work of Jesus Christ upon the cross of Calvary and His bodily resurrection as the completion of His redemptive work on our behalf. This is a vital distinction and shows that seeing miracles is not God's method for transforming human hearts.

The theme of sign and wonders permeates this whole gospel. In John 4:48, the Lord says rather accusingly: "Except ye see signs and wonders, ye will not believe."

B. The Response of the 5,000

Another passage pointing out the same principle is John 6:2, "And a great multitude followed him, because they saw his miracles which he did on them that were diseased." Here you have a great multitude following Jesus because of all the miracles that took place before their very eyes. They were obviously convinced that this was the greatest miracle worker the world had ever seen and they were not disappointed.

In the following verses we have the report of the miracle of the feeding of the 5,000 which John again calls a sign.

The Gospel of John is the book in the New Testament where the word, "sign" ("semeion" in the Greek) occurs most frequently.

After feeding this multitude, no skeptic is left. There is total "faith" in Jesus. Look at verse 14: "Then those men, when they had seen the miracle that Jesus did, said, This is of a truth that prophet that should come into the world."

The multitude wanted to elect Him as their king. A man who could multiply bread with His mere word was the obvious man of the hour to meet the needs of the nation on every physical level.

Was Jesus convinced that their faith was genuine? He withdrew from them, as we can read in the following verse 15: "When Jesus therefore perceived that they would come and take him by force, to make him a king, he departed again into a mountain himself alone."

Notice also what Jesus said to this crowd in verse 26: "Ye seek me, not because ye saw the miracles, but because ye did eat of the loaves, and were filled." For the sake of carnal, selfish desire in order to have their senses gratified and their physical needs met they were ready to follow Jesus.

The Lord told them what their deficiency was: "He who comes to me shall never hunger" (verse 35). In other words, "He who comes to me in genuine spiritual faith will never hunger spiritually."

Note verse 36: "But I said unto you, that ye also have seen me, and believe not." Seeing, then, is not believing.

Absorbing reality through the five senses, even witnessing spectacular miracles as recorded in the Gospels, is not equivalent in God's sight to genuine, soul-transforming faith.

Look at verses 29 and 30 where the Lord declared how all miracles should culminate in true belief in Him. Although they had just witnessed this unique event of feeding the 5,000, they had the boldness to ask (verse 30): "...What sign shewest thou then, that we may see, and believe thee?" In other words, these people were essentially miracle mongers. As long as they could see miracles, they were ready to believe. They wanted to see first and then believe, but the Lord declares in the same Gospel: "Blessed are they that have not seen and yet have believed" (20:29).

The Lord wanted to introduce the multitude of His followers to the true spiritual meaning of His signs. "You must eat of my flesh and drink of my blood," said Jesus in the same chapter. In other words, "I must be everything to you, not only your physical sustainer." The Greek word for sign, "semeion," points to something beyond. It is like a signpost and never the goal itself. Where the signpost becomes the goal itself, people are misled.

So Jesus said, "I am the light of the world" and healed the man born blind (John 9). He said, "I am the resurrection and the life" and raised Lazarus from the dead (John 11). He explained that He was the bread of life and fed the 5,000. Why? In order that we might believe that the hungry would be supernaturally fed and the blind would see and the dead would be raised? We know how this in no way corresponds to reality.

These signs were rather a pointer to the goal of believing in the Word of the Lord; namely, that He is the light of the world, the resurrection and the life and bread of life, spiritually speaking. From this structure, one can see that this Gospel, among other things, shows how the Word replaces the sign.

If we don't learn this spiritual lesson, then one has observed signs and wonders in vain. The multitude following Christ should understand these conclusions, in order to receive real spiritual life. However, since they concentrate on the visible world, because of their desire for signs and wonders, they take offense.

"Many therefore of his disciples, when they heard this, said, This is an hard saying; who can hear it?" (John 6:60). The Lord replies: "It is the spirit that quickeneth, the flesh profiteth noth-ing" (verse 63a). The flesh, especially that which appeals to my senses, is of no use. The Spirit gives life. Where is the Spirit now? So many, today, are speaking about the Holy Spirit and spiritual leading. The answer is in the same verse. "The words that I speak unto you, they are spirit, and they are life."

The Word of God and the Holy Spirit are inseparable. The charismatic enthusiast often places himself with his appeal to the Spirit above the Word itself. The Bible does not teach that.

Immediately after Jesus' statement, that His words are spirit and life, there follows one of the most tragic verses of the New Testament. In verse 66 we can see the result of the lack of spir-itual understanding amongst even His disciples, "From that time many of his disciples went back, and walked no more with him." What a tragic development.

Then the Lord asks: "Will you also go away?" (verse 67). In other words, "Is this all you are interested in? Am I only your miracle-worker, whom you follow as long as it pleases your flesh? Are you only looking for sensationalism? Am I only a circus performer to you? Is this what you are following me for?"

And Peter, giving his famous answer, does *not* say: "Lord, to whom shall we go? Thou hast the signs and wonders we need," but "Thou hast the words of eternal life" (verse 68).

Do we see the difference here? Few, the minority, stayed with our Lord because of Himself and His Word. "He that has my commandments, and keepeth them, he it is that loveth me" (John 14:21).

In our days, it is not the majority of Christendom that remains with the Lord because of faithfulness toward His Word. We see many leaving the basis of the Word and follow-ing ecumenical promises and also within the Charismatic Movement, very many are following after a wrong emphasis on signs and wonders.

As both groups turn their back unknowingly on the true Christ revealed in His infallible Word, they are often joining together.

C. The Response of the Apostles

Now, another passage should be mentioned in this respect. In John 20:8 we read about the Apostle John on the morning of the resurrection: "Then went in also that other disciple, which came first to the sepulchre, and he saw, and believed." Now this caught my attention because in the same chapter we read: "Blessed are they that have not seen, and yet have believed" (verse 29).

Why is it the other way round here? The answer is given in the following verse 9: "For as yet they knew not the Scripture, that he must rise again from the dead."

Here, in black and white, without being unduly dogmatic, we read how he had to see, because he didn't yet understand the Scripture. What does this mean? The more I know the Word of God and search the Scriptures, the less I need to walk by sight. The desire for signs and wonders is a sign of spiritual immaturity. "But when I became a man, I put away childish things," Paul declares in another passage, "We walk by faith, not by sight" (2nd Corinthians 5:7).

John 20:29, in connection with Thomas, has been mentioned previously, "Blessed are they that have not seen, and yet have believed." Did Jesus really mean what he said? Is such a statement possible? This is the most dynamic denunciation ever uttered by our Lord of the increasingly popular approach to God by visible miracles.

Peter was there in this upper room and heard that statement. Later he wrote to a group of Christians in Asia Minor who had never been to Palestine, nor had they seen Jesus. He wrote to them in his first epistle: "Whom having not seen, ye love; in whom, though now ye see him not, yet believe" (1st Peter 1:8).

Looking back to John 20:29, where the famous statement of our Lord to Thomas is mentioned, the subsequent verses must be understood in their context. "And many other signs truly did Jesus in the presence of his disciples, which are not written in this book: But these are written, that ye might believe that Jesus is the Christ, the Son of God; and that believing ye might have life through his name" (verses 30–31).

Clearly this passage shows how the Word replaces the initial function of the sign, that is, pointing to Jesus, "But these (signs) are written, that ye might believe."

So God had a plan (verse 30) when He selected 8 signs from all the deeds of Jesus. They all culminated in the Word of God.

And the Lord tells us in the Bible that His Spirit is fully capable of taking God's spoken or written Word and driving it so deep into the center of man's personal being, into his very heart, that he is able to know and even love God, in order to bring about this spiritual revolution which the Bible calls the new birth or real faith in Jesus, "...and that believing ye might have life through his name" (verse 31b).

D. Which is the Greatest Wonder?

In addition, this is the greatest miracle according to Biblical teaching. Therefore, it does not say there is joy in heaven when a blind man sees or a lame man walks, but rather when a sinner repents. Only he receives eternal life, for even Lazarus had to die again.

This contains also the answer to an often misquoted verse used a proof text for sign gifts today; namely, John 14:12, "Verily, verily, I say unto you, He that believeth on me, the works that I do shall he do also; and greater works than these shall he do."

The greatest miracle is the new birth, which is possible because of Calvary and the events of Pentecost. In this we also believe in the God of miracles. This presentation should not be misunderstood as saying that there are no more miracles from God today.

It depends on your perspective: Whoever lives by faith will see miracle upon miracle. Each answer to prayer is a wonder. I believe it is a greater miracle when someone with an occultic or drug background begins the victorious life of sanctification, than is the healing of a lame person.

Even in a certain sense when we have a similar situation to the Book of Acts, that is where hardly any revelation of God through His Word is present, God can compensate this lack by supernatural intervention.

In this way, God provided manna for the children of Israel in the wilderness, since sowing and reaping was not possible in the desert. However, the manna ceased when Israel entered the Promised Land, for then it was possible to reap a harvest in a normal way, for God does not support laziness.

Many pastors and teachers do not give the full counsel of God and yet we find them giving extra-Biblical revelation.

It is foolish to seek special revelation if we already have the full counsel of God in the Bible.

Luke reports how Herod Antipas, when seeing Jesus, "was exceeding glad...and hoped to have seen some miracle done by him. Then he questioned him [Jesus] in many words; but he [Jesus] answered him nothing" (Luke 23:89).

Why did the Lord remain silent? God had already spoken clearly to Herod through John the Baptist. We read that Herod liked to listen to him.

Nevertheless, Herod had John the Baptist beheaded and thus eliminated the source through whom God had spoken to him. When Jesus stood before Herod, God had nothing more to tell him.

It is foolish, if not outright dangerous, to seek after signs and special revelations, when God already has revealed everything through His Word and when we have the Bible for our use.

SIGNS IN ACTS

In the Book of Acts, the attentive reader will notice that the words, "signs and wonders," in the report about Paul's *first* missionary journey, occur quite frequently.

In the passage about Paul's *second* journey, they are not even mentioned once.

In the *third* missionary journey, we see evidence of supernatural events. However, in general, a tendency toward their decreasing use can be observed. The same apostle who could supernaturally heal the sick in Ephesus, wrote in his farewell letter that he left Trophimus sick in Miletum (2nd Timothy 4:20). He obviously could not heal anymore.

One gets the impression in Acts that God gave authenticity to his apostles in the early stages in a visible way. In chapter 5, we read of the first openly committed sin in this new era of the church, a lie from Ananias and Sapphira, which God publically judged with death. If this was the standard today, who of us would still be alive?

The Lord confirmed the new revelation of the apostles with signs. Now, we are established upon the foundation of the apostles and prophets (Ephesians 2:20). Certainly you can only lay a foundation once. The demand for signs and wonders in our day implies a new claim to revelation. As Whitcomb points out, this would be a colossal step backward and downward to the foundation phase. Instantly all of our Bibles would be incomplete.

We read of John the Baptist, the greatest of all those born of a woman, that he didn't perform any miracles (John 10:41). Why? Was he lacking in spiritual power? Not at all; rather, he was filled with the Holy Spirit from the womb. However, he was the last prophet of the Old Covenant and therefore had no new revelation.

Again, we see the difference between a sign and a miracle. Every sign in the New Testament is a miracle. Yet in contrast to the latter, it has a far-reaching fulfillment. Therefore, we speak of the sign, and not the miracle, of Jonah.

It is a miracle to survive in the stomach of a fish, but, because this event points to the resurrection of our Lord, it is referred to as a sign.

If signs were normal today, as many are demanding, then God would have something new to reveal. Again we would have to leave the foundation of "sola Scriptura," because our Bibles would be incomplete.

Divine healing does not occur today as a demonstration for unbelievers. Rather, the Lord has transferred the matter of healing in the church to that as described in James 5:13–16.

It is my firm conviction that God is healing some sick Christians today, but in a very different way than He did when Christ was here, and for a very different purpose.

In James 5, it says that the sick Christian shall ask for the elders of the church to come to him. God does not accomplish it through a faith healer or in spectacular form. According to Romans 8:23, "We are waiting for the redemption of our body." Our bodies are therefore not yet redeemed and because of that also suffer from sickness.

FROM SIGN TO SCRIPTURE

This development from signs to the Word, from the visible to the invisible, can be seen in the epistles. Peter describes in his second letter how they had seen the glory of Jesus. "...but we were eyewitnesses of His majesty" (2nd Peter 1:16). He doesn't encourage us to seek that which is visible, but, on the contrary, to search the Scriptures: "We also have a more sure word of prophecy..." (1:19).

Similarly, John testifies in his first epistle that he saw, heard and touched the Word of life, "And these things write we unto you, that your joy may be full" (1st John 1:4). We should rejoice on account of the Word of God.

No one should appear to deny that God can perform miracles at any time that He wishes. He is sovereign and free to do so, and has done so, according to His plan. The question is whether a ministry of signs and wonders is normative or a standard of God's work among men in all ages. As pointed out, if miraculous signs are normative, would they not cease to be signs?

SIGNS, WONDERS AND MIRACLES
We would like to summarize the 5 passages in the Scriptures where the three Greek terms "semeion," "teras," and "dynamis" are used.

The King James Bible translates the word "dynamis" differently. In Acts 2:22, it is rendered as "miracle;" as "power" in Romans 15:19; and as "mighty deed" in 2nd Corinthians 12:12.

When these three words occur together in the same verse or context, regardless of the sequence, this does not refer to one particular event, rather to something like a current or a movement over a larger time span.

The first passage is Acts 2:22. The Messiah performed these miracles. Romans 15:19 is the next text and indicates that these words refer to apostolic events, since Paul writes in the following verse that he "strived to preach the gospel, not where Christ was named." However, it is a bit ambiguous.

In the third passage, 2nd Corinthians 12:12, Paul declares that "…the signs of an apostle were wrought among you in all patience, in signs and wonders and mighty deeds." It is beyond doubt. So these signs were apostolic.

We do read, for example in Acts, how Philip evangelized with obvious success in Samaria. Many Samaritans believed without receiving the Holy Spirit. Only as the apostles from Jerusalem came and laid their hands on them, did they receive the Holy Spirit.

We are faced with the question: "Why couldn't Philip lay his hands on the Samaritans? Because he was a deacon and not an apostle.

Every person who appeals to this passage to justify "Biblically" his act of transferring the Holy Spirit by laying on hands actually implies, often unknowingly, that he is an apostle. However, the apostles knew the Lord after the flesh, but this particular time is long past. A similar thought is expressed in 2nd Corinthians 5:16.

The next verse which I want to mention is Hebrews 2:4. This passage, especially in connection with the previous verse, is the strongest Biblical argument for the supernatural powers belonging to the time of the early church.

We can see from the whole of Scripture that the Lord usually confirms His work with two or three witnesses. In verses 3 and 4 we see the three witnesses of the New Covenant. The first one is the Lord Jesus, "...which at the first began to be spoken by the Lord..." (Hebrews 2:3).

He is followed by the apostles, who confirmed the preaching of the Word in their capacity as eyewitnesses, "...and was confirmed unto us by them that heard him (verse 3).

The third witness is God himself, "God also bearing them witness, both with the signs and wonders, and with divers miracles."

Is God still working like this today? The predicate (verb) of the main sentence, the word confirmed or attested in Hebrews 2:3, in the Greek, is clearly in a past tense. The writer of the epistle to the Hebrews was already using a past tense, aorist.

The fourth verse, although it is in the present tense, yet as a so-called "genitive absolute," refers to the time of the tense of the main clause in the previous verse. This explains why God worked mainly in the beginning through wonders and signs.

The fifth and last passage is 2nd Thessalonians 2:9. This passage, in particular, is dealing with the events preceding the

Second Coming of Christ. We can therefore expect the occurrence of signs and wonders, which God initially used to confirm His word, once again. In this respect, the Charismatic
Movement is a fulfillment of God's Word. Even if we had
never heard of the Pentecostal or Charismatic Movement,
Biblical prophecy alone would lead us to the conclusion that
the occurrence and spread of the above-mentioned phenomena
at the end of the church Age would happen.

But, unlike the second chapter of Hebrews, its origin will
not be found in God, but, according to 2nd Thessalonians 2:9,
is definitely in Satan. The history of the Pentecostal and
Charismatic Movement reveals this very clearly too.

At first sight, we might be tempted to draw parallels. It
looks like the early church — the same terms are used — but
behind all this is a completely different source. This explains
why many counselors, who have tested tongues and have had
a chance to look behind the scenes of what seemed very
Biblical and pious at first impression, found the root usually in
the occult.

Again, we understand why charismatics will quote the passages of Acts 2, 8, 10 and 19 to confirm their position. But
these passages report historical breakthroughs which God,
according to Hebrews 2:3–4, accompanied with signs and
wonders.

From this parallel we also understand why the Charismatic
Movement is growing rapidly. Especially in countries with
much spiritism (England, South America and other Catholic
countries) these tongue movements, due to their spiritualistic
source, have great impact and influence.

As we draw nearer to the return of the Lord Jesus, signs
such as tongues, healings and miraculous manifestations will
increase in frequency.

Yet, it is unfortunately a consequent fulfillment in a negative
respect: the manifestation of strong delusions which are named

significantly almost straight after verse 9 of 2nd Thessalonians
2.

SIGNS AND THE LAST DAYS

These connections explain why the expression "signs and wonders" in the Biblical passages which deal with the return of
Christ are always mentioned in connection with deceit. The
words in Greek for the miracles of Jesus and the apostles are
the same as for the miracles of the deceivers. Even in this
respect, wonders wrought by Satan resemble apostolic miracles so closely.

Think of Matthew 24:24 or 2nd Thessalonians 2:9 which
were quoted above. We read about the false prophet, that "he
deceiveth them that dwell on the Earth by the means of those
miracles" (Revelation 13:14). See also Revelation 19:20, or
16:14, "For they are the spirits of devils, working miracles."

Even others who are not true children of God can perform
signs and wonders in the name of Jesus. Let us not forget the
exhortation of our Lord in the Sermon on the Mount, "Many
(not few) will say to me in that day, Lord, have we not prophesied in thy name? and in thy name have cast out devils? and
in thy name have done so many wonderful works? And then
will I profess unto them, I never knew you" (Matthew 7:
22–23).

Our Lord condemned the yearning for signs and wonders.
"...An evil and adulterous generation seeketh after a sign..."
(Matthew 12:39). We have become an evil and adulterous generation, at least in the Western World, and consequently the
desire for signs and wonders is rampant.

As we have tried to point out, the use of signs and wonders
is not the real method to change a man's heart which can be
evil and yet seeking the supernatural at the same time.

Likewise, we read in John 12:37 this seemingly incredible
statement, "But though he (Jesus) had done so many miracles

before them, yet they believed not on him." But Romans 10:17 tells us that faith comes not by seeing, but by hearing the Word of God. Yet for many in our days, "Seeing is believing," although that is not what the Bible says (Hebrews 11:1).

SIGNS IN OUR DAYS
"And many false prophets shall rise, and shall deceive many," the Lord Jesus said in His sermon about His Second Coming (Matthew 24:11). One of the characteristics of the false movements will be that they have tremendous success and results. "They shall deceive many."

The pastor of the world's largest church is Paul Yonggi Cho. He also can claim amazing signs and wonders, but from which source does he receive his power?

Dave Hunt's book, *The Seduction of Christianity* caused quite a stir in the American Christian scene. To some extent, it deals with the teachings of Yonggi Cho. Therefore, I would like to quote some of the book's most interesting statements.

Hunt writes:

> Anyone who imagines that because he thinks certain thoughts or speaks certain words, God must respond in a certain way, has slipped into sorcery, and if not playing God, is at the very least attempting to manipulate God.... Yonggi Cho declares: "By the spoken word we create our universe of circumstances...you create the presence of Jesus with your mouth...He is bound by our lips and by our words...."[39]

> Nowhere in the Bible does it indicate or even imply that the people of God are to use the same methods or power as the pagans. Yonggi Cho; however, not only says that miracles must all conform to his "Law of the Fourth Dimension," but that anyone, including occultists, can "apply the law of the fourth dimension and...perform miracles."

Nevertheless, Pastor Cho assures us that he learned this from "the Holy Spirit" when he asked in prayer why occultists could do miracles just like Christians.

Cho commends the Japanese Buddhist occultists, the Soka Gakkai, for performing "miracles" through visualizing "a picture of prosperity, repeating phrases over and over and developing the human spiritual fourth dimension." And he scolds Christians for not doing likewise....

Unfortunately, much popular teaching in the church today, instead of refuting Eastern mysticism, seems to support it. One example is Yonggi Cho's teaching about his "fourth dimension."[40]

In his attempt to manufacture examples from the Bible for the technique of visualization, Pastor Cho's Biblical exegesis is pure fantasy.

Although he probably does not realize it, Pastor Cho has laid out basic occult theory, an apologetic for nature religion, or witchcraft...

In his sequel to *The Fourth Dimension*, Pastor Cho writes: "We've got to learn how...to visualize and dream the answer as being completed as we go to the Lord in prayer. We should always try to visualize the end result as we pray. In that way, with the power of the Holy Spirit, we can incubate that which we want God to do for us..."

The main thing is that we should know the importance of visualization. If visualization is so all-important, one would expect that the Bible would have a great deal to say about it. But in fact the word does not occur even once in the entire Bible....

However, at this point it should be clearly understood that the whole idea of visualizing a vivid image in the mind in order to produce an effect in the physical world is not just missing from the Bible but is present in all occultic literature as far back as we can go (and is in fact one of the most basic shamanistic devices).

Yet it is being taught not only in the way Cho uses it, but also by Christian psychologists in therapy and by success-motivation teachers, and is the major technique used for inner healing or healing of the memories and even for healing at a distance.[41]

It should be noted that John Wimber gathered much "inspiration" from Yonggi Cho.

Peter Wagner, who introduced John Wimber to Fuller Theological Seminary, received his "Spirit baptism" from Yonggi Cho.

The same principles are applied by many faith healers, but also by Dennis and Rita Bennett and Larry Christenson and have mainly been practiced by the late Agnes Sanford. According to Dave Hunt,

"...Perhaps no women in this century has had a larger influence upon the Christianity of today than prolific best-selling author and teacher Agnes Sanford."[42]

In her book, *The Healing Light,* she writes the following:

"His angels and spiritual messengers are also working through us, and it is often given to us to be conscious of their cooperation and support.

"The spirits of those for whom we have prayed on Earth are working through us....

"...As we pray for His indwelling and for the cooperation of His saints, we become aware of an inrush of power. Some of us feel an actual current of life entering into the centre of the body and rising through the spine. So forceful is this vibration or stream of life that we are forced to keep the

spine erect and the breathing light and even. For a little time
we cannot speak. We are so filled with the fullness of Christ
that there is within no room for words."[43]

This is clearly spiritism. Dave Hunt goes on to say:

> To use imagery effectively in healing the sick, says Agnes
> Sanford, "mental training" is required to develop "the cre-
> ative faculty, that part of the creative imagination that is most
> like God." This is the teaching of Christian Science and other
> mind-science cults. Unfortunately, it is also what Yonggi
> Cho teaches in *The Fourth Dimension*.[44]

Simon, from Acts 8:9, proposed to be something great, because
he was a sorcerer. Let us conclude this subject with the following statement by Dave Hunt:

> Whether practiced by Christians or non-Christians, visualiza-
> tion is purely an occult technique offering a substitute source
> of power, knowledge, and healing, which, if it could be real-
> ized, would make man a god in his own right, independent of
> his Creator.[45]

When we read such statements, it reminds us of the first lie in
the history of mankind: "You will be like God!" That is how
deceit started, and is how seduction will end.

A FINAL CONSIDERATION

Jesus spoke of a man who insisted on seeing in order to
believe. It is the tragic story in Luke chapter 16; of the rich man
who went to the place of torment prepared for those who have
died without genuine faith in the living God.

This rich man now wanted to evangelize, as he knew all too
well how terrible condemnation is. So he asked Abraham to

send Lazarus to his five brethren in order that he, by a spectacular appearance from the dead, might shock them out of their sinful complacency to recognize the reality of God. What do you think of that plan to reach man? Doubtlessly spectacular, but totally outside of God's methods.

Abraham, speaking for God, said to the rich man: "They have Moses and the prophets; let them hear them" (verse 29). So, they have God's written Word.

"No," the rich man replied [in effect], "if one went unto them from the dead, if they could have empirical, visional, tangible evidence to their senses, then they would believe." This answer shows exactly why the rich man was where he was. He despised God's Word. In other words, he declares: "The Bible is good, but not good enough. We need signs and wonders and then they will believe."

This suggestion came directly from the pit (Hades). Then it is prophesied to us that in the last days, the powers of Hades will be let loose upon the world (Revelation 6:8).

Occultism and spiritualism in the Western World is vastly increasing, for example, in Germany where the spiritists have enlarged their numbers by more than one million adherents in recent times.

Exactly parallel to this are the suggestions that signs and wonders must accompany our preaching and healing and should always follow our ministry.

I have before me a quotation from *Christianity Today*:

> One observer estimated that 80 percent of Korea's Christian minority conduct services for the dead covertly, but that it is simply passed over in the churches.[46]

This is the reason why Yonggi Cho is so successful with his magically spiritualistic methods. This is the reason why the Charismatic Movement and the so-called "Third Wave," as a parallel to the increasing occultism and spiritualism, are flourishing as well.

That is the true reason why faith healers like Reinhard Bonnke, John Wimber, Benny Hinn and many, many others have so much success. This is not any kind of spiritual awakening, but rather Hades in sheep's clothing.

Back to the story of the rich man: Abraham said to him, and with this the conversation ended according to Jesus: "If they hear not Moses and the prophets, neither will they be persuaded, though one rose from the dead" (verse 31).

Spiritual truths travel by the mind, not by feelings. "So then faith comes by hearing, and hearing by the word of God" (Romans 10:17).

The Bible declares with special reference to the last days: "Men of corrupt minds, reprobate concerning the faith" (2nd Timothy 3:8). It is the Greek word, "nous," which is rendered "mind" here. It is this "nous" that must be enlightened by the Word of God. "But he that received seed into the good ground is he that heareth the word, and understandeth it" (Matthew 13:23).

Let us be satisfied with the wonderful Word of God, for in the same chapter in which our Lord warns about deceptive signs and wonders (Matthew 24:24), He also declares: "Heaven and Earth shall pass away, but my words shall not pass away" (verse 35).

Point 6

THE SECOND COMING

A COMPLETELY FALSE VIEW OF THIS IS TAUGHT.
The Bible does not teach that there will be a world-wide
revival during the time just prior to the Second Coming of
Christ, but a world-wide deception mainly through signs and
wonders. Again, the epistles speak of a falling away of the
church toward the end of the age of grace (2nd Thessalonians
2:3), "...giving heed to seducing spirits and doctrine of devils"
(1st Timothy 4:1).

Many people begin to nurture their dreams and so, instead
of watching and praying as the Lord so often exhorts us to do,
they are not alert and discerning.

The apostles prophesy the coming of "perilous times" (2nd
Timothy 3:1); "false teachers and damnable heresies" (2nd
Peter 2:1); error (3:3); and teachers of fables (2nd Timothy
4:3–4).

The Gospels predict an increase of unbelief and false
prophets (Matthew 24:11–12), even a real decline of faith
(Luke 18:8). Jesus' response to the question of His Second
Coming was a warning against deception (Matthew 24:4).

In the light of all this, it seems out of place that the current
emphasis is on world-wide revival, charismatic super-spirituality and even on Kingdom or Dominion Theology.

Point 7

RENEWAL THEOLOGY

T HIS IS THE EXEGETICALLY UNTENABLE INTERPRETATION
THAT THE PROPHECY OF JOEL IS AN EVENT TO BE
EXPECTED FOR THE CLOSING OF THE CHURCH AGE.

In order to maintain the unbiblical doctrine of the world-
wide revival of the endtimes, Acts 2:17–18 is quoted again and
again in connection with the prophecy of the prophet Joel.
Now the first partial-fulfillment of this prophecy actually took
place at Pentecost, with the beginning of the church.

First of all, it should be mentioned, that the secret of the
church is not revealed in the Book of Acts but in the epistles
(Ephesians 3:1–5), and here we not only fail to find a message
of revival at the end of the church Age, but we are shown the
exact opposite. It would be possible to quote at least seven
Bible passages which show the whole spectrum starting with
the deception to the falling away in the latter times.

To try to neutralize these clear statements with falsely interpreted passages from the Book of Acts is exegetically not ten-
able and is intellectually dishonest. As we all know, we ought
to interpret the Bible with the Bible.

First, the Lord Jesus does not say one word about revival in
these passages that concern His Second Coming (Matthew 24,
Luke 21). As mentioned above, He speaks of persecution,
deception, and in verse 12 of the exact opposite; namely, the
prevalence not of faith, but of unbelief.

Secondly, when the Apostle Peter mentions these verses of
the Old Testament, he is in Jerusalem.

In this connection let us think of Zechariah 12:10 where it
is emphasized that "the Lord will pour upon the inhabitants of
Jerusalem the spirit of grace...." The apostle initiated the
church first of all in Israel for the Jews. He does not quote this
passage from Joel when he is speaking to the gentiles. He primarily prophesies for his people (Acts 3:26) in that he bridges
over the millennia and combines these two events of the first
and second outpouring of the Spirit.

Zechariah 12:10 shows how prophecy can have a twofold fulfillment. We generally understand this verse to be the conversion of the remnant of the people of Israel, which still lies ahead of us. But the evangelist John also quotes this verse concerning the crucifixion of Jesus (John 19:37), that is, Jesus first coming.

Now the question is, "When does this second outpouring of the Spirit take place?" Here again one must interpret the Bible with the Bible. When we look at the other verses (Isaiah 32:14-18, Ezekiel 11:17-19, 36:24-29 and so on), which speak of this event, then we can understand that the prophesied second outpouring of the Spirit stands in connection with the gathering of the people of Israel, and probably coincides with the beginning of the Millennium.

For instance, Ezekiel 39:28-29 states: "Then they shall know that I am the Lord their God, which caused them to be led into captivity among the heathen: but I have gathered them unto their own land and have left none of them any more there.

"Neither will I hide my face any longer from them: for I have poured out my spirit upon the house of Israel, saith the Lord God."

Characteristically, the famous passage in Joel is found between promises of (Joel 2:27) and events centered round Israel (Joel 2: 32, 3:1-3).

Thirdly, according to Ephesians 3:15 and Colossians 1:26, the future dispensation of grace was not revealed to any of the prophets of the Old Testament (Matthew 11:13, Luke 16:16), as we have briefly mentioned above. They prophesied the future blessings of Israel. The events foreseen in Acts 2:19-20 come to fulfillment in Revelation 6:12; that is the apocalyptic events in the Tribulation period.

A second outpouring of the Spirit of God will take place over the remnant of Israel (Isaiah 10:21-22); the inhabitants of Jerusalem (Zechariah 12:10). The verses immediately before that passage in Zechariah show the judgement of the nations and the events around Israel, that is, Jerusalem.

It is also evident that Israel stands apart from the Law, under the disposition of signs, but the church, first of all, under the Word of God.

Fourthly, according to Romans 11:25, the nation of Israel will not be converted during this present dispensation of grace. Yet, God has promised the salvation of all Israel (Romans 11:26).

Therefore, it is obvious that the Lord will again intervene in a special way, though not during the time of the nations any more, but in relation to His people of the Old Covenant.

In any case, these events are still in the future. The Holy Spirit has long since been poured out abundantly for today's dispensation of grace (Titus 3:5–6), and the church has not to wait for a second Pentecost but for the return of the Lord Jesus Christ.

In order to prevent any misunderstanding, I should like to say that the impression should not arise that I am against revivals. On the contrary, we hope, pray and believe that the Lord will still be working locally in a mighty way. For instance, one can only praise God for what He is doing in China. However, to expect a global, world-wide revival is unbiblical.

The thing that makes the Charismatic Movement so doubtful and suspect to me is the observation that almost all Pentecostal circles usually quote this passage in Joel, or the verses in Acts 2 connected with it, as a Biblical evidence for their emphasis on, and unfolding of, just such remarkable gifts.

That is, so to speak, the written proof. Wherever one goes, people are referring to this passage in Joel. It is considered to be the basis for the manifestation of such peculiar events today. This is how it is taught, sung, printed and disseminated repeatedly. But we have just shown how these passages, at least in the second or complete fulfillment of them, have really nothing to do with the church at all.

Here, I would like to appeal to intellectual sincerity. Isn't the following question justified? "When the headline of a subject is already incorrect, then how can that which follows be much better or accurate?"

Visions, for example, which are based on the passage in Acts 2, are therefore to be "considered" with the greatest caution, as well as the people who are referring to these verses for their prophesies (Zechariah 13:2).

The late Ralph Shallis, former British missionary to France, wrote to me saying that he could see the judgement of God over the churches in the "Charismatic Renewal" (1st Peter 4:17), because the believers would rather seek after sensations and religious bliss, the way of pleasing the flesh, and less and less after the cross of Christ. In fact, he came to this conclusion after studying this subject in Isaiah 33:19.

You will see those arrogant people no more, those people of an obscure speech, with their strange, incomprehensible tongue (NIV).

When I think of some statements in Paul's first letter to the Corinthians, especially in chapter 11:17ff, then I am inclined to agree with him more and more. Very often, the Bible knowledge of many is so superficial that it is not through the Word of God but through personalities and experiences that believers are controlled, if not manipulated.

God permits spiritual darkness to be sent in judgement (Judges 9:23, Isaiah 29:9–10). Today we observe, in a sense, foreshadowing events that lead to the outpouring of God's wrath in the Tribulation (Revelation 16), a "pouring out" of deceitful spirits (1st Timothy 4:1).

When we think that, in regard of the endtimes, the Bible even speaks of strong delusions (2nd Thessalonians 2:11) which God will send, and Scripture admonishes us repeatedly to be sober, then a Bible-true Christian really ought to recognize what is going on.

As a whole, especially in the Western World, we are not facing "revival" but the infiltration of the church in the endtimes.

Point 8

THE HOLY SPIRIT AND THE LORD JESUS

IT IS NOT THE LORD JESUS WHO IS SPOKEN OF PRIMARILY, BUT THE SPIRIT.

The Holy Spirit is mentioned very frequently in the charismatic circles. One often has the impression that it is not the Lord Jesus any more, but the Holy Spirit who has become the central figure.

Even if we are only slightly acquainted with Scripture, we realize that the Holy Spirit does not wish to be the center (John 15:26), nor does He want to speak of Himself (John 16:13). He desires to make the Lord Jesus the central point and to glorify Him (John 16:14). The Holy Spirit works, as someone has said, like a searchlight who illuminates the person of the Lord Jesus and is not visible Himself. Also, according to John 16:8–11, the Spirit of God works primarily to lead people to repentance. But many today have become proud through their gifts.

Point 9

THE ECUMENICAL ALIGNMENT

Today we are living in the age where preparations are being made for the appearance of the Antichrist. The Bible reveals to us that the Antichrist will receive world-wide worship when he appears in his deceptively religious garment.

As has already been pointed out, this deception is made possible through signs and wonders. The coming of the false messiah will presumably be initiated by a world-wide "revival" (Revelation 13:8) based on supernatural phenomena.

When we observe the increasing number of Roman Catholics who receive the "baptism of the spirit" and how many a Protestant and even evangelicals feel themselves drawn toward the Catholics because of tongue-speaking, and when we see big "fraternization scenes" between Protestants and Roman Catholics on the basis of "gifts of grace," then we realize that the possibility of a charismatic "superchurch" is not a strange thought any more. In the coming massive effort of a world-wide evangelization called "Evangelization 2,000" Catholics and charismatic evangelicals plan to cooperate closely.

At the North American Congress on the Holy Spirit in New Orleans Superdome, in July 1987, Vinson Synan, congress chairman, stated:

> If you want to see something beautiful, come see a Spirit-filled Catholic mass.[47]

Though officially billed primarily as a Pentecostal/charismatic gathering, it was overwhelmingly Catholic in its orientation. At least 50 % of those attending were Roman Catholic.

According to Biblical prophecy there will be, in the last days, a great world-wide church which the Word of God calls "Babylon the Great" (Revelation 17:5).

Many Bible scholars see in the Roman Catholic Church a system which has definite parallels to the Babylonian cult.

The most obvious interpretation seems to be that this "Superchurch," a fusion of the Ecumenical Movement and Rome, will be made up of all the apostatized Christians (not only from the Catholic church) throughout the world.

It is important, alongside such statements, to differentiate between the doctrine and the person. There are Catholics who no doubt fear God. The above statement does not mean that there are no reborn believers in the Catholic church.

However, the Roman church, as a system, is definitely un-Biblical.

It can be clearly observed how the Charismatic Movement is shifting more and more toward the Roman system. In doing so it is providing a bridgehead from Protestantism to Catholicism.

Philip Potter, former General Secretary of the ecumenical World Council of churches in Geneva, said:

> The Charismatic renewal is the bond between the churches of the Reformation, the Roman Catholic Church, the conservative- evangelicals and the Orthodox church.[48]

This becomes even clearer through the following statement:

> Coming directly from a visit to the pope at the Vatican, du Plessis told about his impressions: "You would think the pope is Pentecostal. He talked so much about Pentecost and why one should be baptized and filled."[49]

In the book *Angels on Assignment,* Charles & Francis Hunter write:

> God told me that the pope has neither greater influence than the least Christian, nor greater privileges. However, because of the great influence he has on the people, his election

becomes a matter for God. He has chosen a man named
Karol Wojtyla from Poland to become pope.[50]

Every Bible-believing Christian should be able to recognize
which "God" is spoken of here. The present pope has never
made a secret of the fact that he receives his special power
from the Black Madonna, the national religious symbol of
Poland. On his last visit to Nigeria, he told the people that it is
possible for Muslims and Christians to call themselves brothers in one God.

Such a man has been chosen by God to be pope, according
to *Angels on Assignment*, a pope who is very much involved in
Mariology and shows clear counter-reformatory tendencies.

Protestant missionaries in Catholic countries tell how their
work has become increasingly difficult since John Paul II has
come into office.

The Bible states that the worship of Mary is idolatry and the
Word of God admonishes us not to have fellowship with idol-
aters.

T. W. Cooke writes in a leaflet entitled, *The Gift of Tongues,*

We are living in the latter days, when much of the Spirit's
work is counterfeited.

Consider the following, for instance. In his book, *Catholic
Pentecostals,* Kevin Ranaghan says,

...the baptism of the Spirit leads to a greater love for Mary,
greater veneration for the pope, greater devotion to the
Catholic church, increased regularity at the Mass and more
power in witnessing to these things."

This alone should convince evangelicals that there is more than
one source of spiritual influence, as Rome's ecclesiastical

system cannot be of the Lord. Any manifestation which supports it should be avoided.

Reverend Michael Harper, the well-known Pentecostal of the Anglican church, expresses in his book, *The Three Sisters*, his great desire to see evangelicals, Pentecostals and Catholic charismatics united. What is the end-result of this development? David du Plessis gives the answer:

> What is the Pentecostal position regarding unity with Roman Catholics? Their spokesman, the only man to bear the name Mr. Pentecost says, "nothing less than full ecumenicity." And what is full ecumenicity?...Full ecumenicity means total unity with the Roman Catholic Church and that in the absolute sense.[51]

As already noted, the greatest problem is that more and more churches, which several years ago rejected on Biblical grounds any relationship with Rome, are now enthusiastic about this type of ecumenical fellowship.

One is no longer a "brother" on the basis of the Bible, repentance and the acceptance of God's Word, but on the basis of a charismatic experience.

The tendency is away from God and the Bible toward a humanistic orientation. So man and his experience become the criteria of everything that is "spiritual."

The end result of this process is the dethronement of God and the exaltation of man and his experiences. I would like to quote John Stott again:

> My third example is Pentecostal Christians, many of whom make experience the major criterion of truth...One of the movement's leaders said recently, apropos of the Catholic Pentecostals, that what matters in the end is "not doctrine but experience above the revealed truth of God."[52]

The whole development reminds one of a statement Leonhard
Ravenhill made several years ago:

> Moreover, the Devil has substituted...familiar spirits for the
> Holy Spirit, Christian Science for divine healing, the
> Antichrist for the true Christ, and the church of Rome for the
> true church.[53]

Another parallel to Catholicism can be seen also in Peter
Wagner's article, *Territorial Spirits and World Missions.* In a
positive context he relates the following story under the head-
ing, "Bermuda Triangle":

> Kenneth McAll spent many years as a missionary surgeon in
> China, then returned to England as a consulting psychiatrist.
> In China he began a deliverance ministry and did consid-
> erable research and writing on the subject.
> In 1972, he and his wife were sailing through the
> Bermuda Triangle...They were overpowered by a fierce
> storm, but fortunately they were rescued.
> McAll discovered through his research that in the
> Bermuda Triangle, the slave traders had thrown overboard
> some two million slaves who were either too sick or too
> weak to be sold and then collected insurance for them.
> Sensing that God was leading him to do something,
> McAll recruited several Anglican bishops, priests, and others
> throughout England to celebrate a Jubilee Eucharist in 1977.
> Another was held shortly afterward in Bermuda itself.
> The stated purpose was to seek the "specific release of all
> those who had met their untimely deaths in the Bermuda
> Triangle."
> As a result, the curse was lifted. McAll reported in 1982,
> "From the time of the Jubilee Eucharist until now — five

years — no known inexplicable accidents have occurred in
the Bermuda Triangle."[54]

This is age-old Catholic superstition, a so-called Mass for the
dead.
Peter Wagner is also called "Mr. church Growth." How shall
we interpret this kind of church growth when so little discernment is evident? Peter Wagner goes on to quote the names of
the six demonic principalities allegedly in charge of the U.S.
Their names are: "Ralphes, Anoritho, Manchester, Apolion,
Deviltook and one unnamed."[55]

In the book, *Power Evangelism*, John Armstrong states:

> Wagner even called together a conference at the seminary in
> an effort to get Christian leaders to bind the various demons
> (including the demon of homelessness, the demon of sick-
> ness, and the demon of the Bermuda Triangle)...
>
> In fact, Wagner reports an incident in which unbelievers
> merely passing the stadium in Latin America where power
> evangelist Carlos Annacondia, a Latin American evangelist
> of considerable following, was preaching, were slain in the
> Spirit.[56]

This kind of "spiritual warfare" reverts to a pagan world-view
and leads to a preoccupation with the demonic. Instead of
becoming Christ-centered and enjoying the freedom in the
Lord Jesus, believers end up in magical thinking and become
entangled in religious spiritism and white magic.

In the same vein are the symptoms it produces. Like the
"Toronto Blessing," it often brings about bizarre spectacles. In
Michael Horton's *Power Religion*, we read:

> "Around the world among Christians of various theological
> persuasions," writes John White, are "reports of great weep-

ing or laughter, shaking, extreme terror, visions, falling (or
what is sometimes called 'being slain in the Spirit'), being
'drunk with the Spirit' and other revival experiences."[57]

The "Toronto Blessing" owes its name to a small Vineyard
Fellowship in Toronto, Canada. People are falling down with
various manifestations such as prolonged laughter, symptoms
of drunkenness, rolling on the floor or loss of strength.

In this movement, people like Benny Hinn demonstrate their
"anointing" by *blowing* on the congregation that "falls to the
ground under the power."

The key person is Rodney Howard-Browne, whose spe-
ciality is to command people to *laugh*. For this reason, it is also
called "the laughing revival." Amongst the variety of bizarre
phenomena, the so-called "Holy Spirit laughter" is prominent.
It is noteworthy that in the Bible, when it mentions that God
laughs, it is always associated with judgement.

In Psalm 2, verse 4, it states: "The One enthroned in heaven
laughs; the Lord scoffs at them."

Or in Proverbs, God's Word says: "Since you ignored all my
advice and would not accept my rebuke, I in turn will laugh at
your disaster; I will mock when calamity overtakes you"
(Proverbs 1:25–26). See also Psalm 37:13 and 59:8.

The latest variation of the "Toronto Blessing," the so-called
"Pensacola Revival," has not been exempted from these manifestations, although it is in a more moderate frame.

These phenomena, especially falling backward and being
"slain in the spirit," are also known in paganism, in Hinduism
(there it is called Shakti Pat), hypnotism and mesmerism.

It is an interesting thought that Paul, when describing the
spiritual armor of Ephesians 6, mentions "standing" (Greek
"histamai") three times in verses 11, 13 and 14 (which is in the
imperative).

It is noteworthy that in the spiritual conflict, the Bible uses either the word "resist" (Greek: "anthistamai,") "stand against," James 4:7, 1st Peter 5:9; or "stand" ("histamai").

Some claim to be Spirit-filled, but what we see today is an "army" often found laying on the ground, *falling* when the "spirit" comes instead of *standing*!

In view of the fact that Paul had in mind the armor of a Roman soldier, it would be unthinkable, except in a time of defeat, to see Roman soldiers lying on the ground. Lying on their backs would be like turtles upside down, a hopeless picture of defeat. Peter admonishes in 2nd Peter 3:17, "Therefore...be on your guard so that you may not be carried away by the deceit of wicked men, falling from your secure position."

Peter Wagner, together with John Wimber and Yonggi Cho, are the fathers of the so-called "Third Wave." This "Wave" wants to penetrate into churches and groups which have not yet been influenced by the Charismatic Movement. The connection between Peter Wagner and Yonggi Cho has already been mentioned. Wagner received his "baptism in the Spirit" through Yonggi Cho. The *Dictionary of Pentecostal and Charismatic Movements* relates Cho's conversion as follows:

> Raised as a Buddhist, Paul rejected his religion as he was dying of tuberculosis and aspired to become a medical doctor, but Jesus later appeared to him in the middle of the night dressed as a fireman, called him to preach, and filled him with the Holy Spirit.[58]

Cho's teaching and its relationship to the occult has been dealt with before. It is interesting therefore that Hank Hanegraaff, president of the Christian Research Institute, comes to a similar conclusion:

Cho's concept of fourth-dimensional thinking is nothing short of occultism. In his bestselling book, *The Fourth Dimension*, Cho unveils his departure from historic Christian theology and his entry into the world of the occult.[59]

The Charismatic Movement is not only the cement between the Protestant and the Catholic church, it has the tendency to lead to syncretism.

Arnold Bittlinger ranks as the father of the Charismatic Movement in Germany. Many of his writings are considered to be standard works of this so-called renewal movement in Germany. In an article called *Integrating Other Religious Traditions into Western Christianity*, published by the World Council of churches in 1989, he writes as follows:

In the course of my research work I became interested in the African Independent churches, where I found a fine blend of traditional African and Christian elements.

When I discovered that many charismatic elements in those churches had also roots in the African pre-Christian traditions I began to look for charismatic elements also in other religions.

I discovered that especially the charismata of "healing" and of "prophecy" were sometimes more convincing in those religions than in the charismatic renewal — at least as far as it is influenced by the North American type of Christianity.

In shamanism I found fascinating parallels to the ministry of Jesus, whom I began to understand as an archetype of a shaman. Concerning "healing," I was especially impressed by the holistic approach to healing, which I found among American Indians. This motivated me to to encourage such an approach also for our Christian healing services.

Concerning "prophecy," I am impressed by experiences in Hinduism. Some of our European "prophets" discovered and developed their prophetic gift under the influence of Hindu gurus.

Also other charismatic experiences have their sometimes expressive equivalents in other religious traditions (e.g., "praying in the spirits in Hatha yoga).

I am convinced that the charismatic renewal will become more significant — especially for the mission of the church — if it also takes seriously the charismata of other religions.

Since 1966 I have been involved in the work of an ecumenical academy which is connected with an ecumenical community. A major concern of this work is the development of an ecumenical spirituality....

We also had conferences on the Chinese *I Ching* and on the Tibetan *Bardo Godol*. But our main concern is to go back to our own Celtic and Alemanic traditions and to try to revitalize them in order to integrate them in our Christian belief.[60]

In view of the fact that Arnold Bittlinger has been of such decisive influence with regard to the Neo-pentecostal Movement in Germany, these statements have a sobering effect.

If we now summarize and consider all these distinctive marks, then one can easily and clearly recognize that the Charismatic Movement is a mimicry, a dangerous counterfeit of Satan. It is a movement which is usually promoted by people who, as genuine believers, are to a certain degree infiltrated by deceiving spirits and therefore have hardly any discernment.

It has already been pointed out how the Apostle Paul was complaining to the Corinthians: "...or if you receive another spirit, ...ye might bear with him' (2nd Corinthians 11:4).

But sadly, today, the situation basically looks similar, especially among circles where people base their teaching primarily on the epistle to the Corinthians.

Thanks to the enormous occult revival of our day, a regular pentecost of hell, the number of devotees and members of this movement is growing steadily.

The New Age movement is sympathetic toward these charismatic phenomena and even the Theosophical Society, in their evaluation, underscore the importance of the renewal movement. In a theosophical article called *The Power of Prayer: Recent Trends*, it is stated:

> My experience is that the present charismatic renewal movement is a move by the Christian fellowship toward the ideals set out by H.P. Blavatsky. Admittedly, they assume a personal God, but even that is expanded to a Holy Spirit which we may regard as impersonal.[61]

CONCLUSION

LOOKING UNTO THE LORD JESUS

It must be admitted that this subject, dealing with occult involvement amongst believers, can lead to an unhealthy introspection in an inexperienced and immature believer. Should this book have such an effect on any one reader, then this negative result would have defeated its purpose. This book wants to show how dangerous it is not to walk by faith (2nd Corinthians 5:7), but to heed feelings, experiences, signs and wonders and lastly to concentrate on one's self in a certain degree.

We are to become sober and watchful, but Biblical faith does not look at oneself and the weaknesses of the flesh.

A truly Christian life neither consists of proud sinlessness nor of an unhealthy occupation with our own mistakes. It consists of a trusting obedience toward the known will of God and the loving service toward our fellow man.

Abraham, who did not work one sign, is called the father of all believers in Romans 4:12 and 16. It is said of him that he did not look at himself, his dead body, but he only clung to the promises of God. He held fast the promises of the Lord and therefore only looked unto him. He was his real consolation, the true anchor of his soul (Hebrews 6:19). Through this faith, he became strong and honored God. It was a faith which was established in the unseen world, and which expected everything from God and nothing from itself, a faith which counted on God.

Thus we should not walk by sight or look at ourselves, but walk by faith and lay hold of the promises of God in His wonderful Word; hold fast no matter how positive or negative our feelings or the opinion of the world may be. This kind of faith proves God right and therefore let us look unto the Lord Jesus, the author and finisher of our faith (Hebrews 12:2). He is the true Saviour and Victor over all these powers of darkness. "Mine eyes are ever toward the Lord; for he shall pluck my feet out of the net" (Psalm 25:15). Such faith may claim: "We know that whosoever is born of God sinneth not; but he that is begotten of God keepeth himself, and that wicked one toucheth him not" (1st John 5:18).

Why do these counterfeit movements so strongly infiltrate the believers and churches? If someone accuses us of lack of spiritual power, authority and sanctification, we must honestly and humbly admit the truth of this sad fact and be willing to repent. If I said, "Everything is all right with me," I myself would be a hypocrite.

On the other hand, I tell people who want to offer me a number of shortcuts to spiritual renewal, like laying on of hands, baptism of the Spirit, experience, gifts, visions, et cetera. "The Bible tells only of one occasion where we find the Father quickly moving or running toward His creature." It is the story of the prodigal son. Here we see the occasion where we rapidly receive fullness, authority and God's power.

I cannot forget the question of a godly evangelist: "To whom is the Father running to meet? The great people of the world, the pious ones, the holy ones, the churchgoers?" Or, in relation to our subject, is it the Christian who longs for more spiritual gifts, or baptism of the Spirit, or desires more experiences? No! It is for the sinner who was about to ask for forgiveness. He is the one to whom the Father is running, "Father, I have sinned against heaven, and before thee" (Luke 15:18). That is the way to more spiritual power. This is the way back to the heart of God: Repentance!

In the letters to the seven churches (Revelation 2–3) we have several deplorable situations, but the Lord Jesus rebuked none of the saints of those churches for not having received the baptism of the Spirit or having too few spiritual gifts. However, five times He says, "Repent"!

May the Lord give us grace that we may go the old way of the cross, the way of being broken and of obedience, that we may receive grace, strength and blessing of the Lord so that in these last days we also might be able to overcome and to live a life that gives glory to God and results in fruit and blessings for many.

FOOTNOTE REFERENCES

1. Watchman Nee, *The Latent Power of the Soul*, Christian Fellowship Publishers, p.34.

2. *Be Filled with the Holy Spirit*, a lecture given in Germany by Alfred Kuen, translated.

3. Michael Griffiths, *Three men filled with the Spirit*, Overseas Missionary Fellowship, p.3839, 1969.

4. Spiros Zodhiates, *Tongues*, Ridgefield AMG Press, p.70.

5. John Stott, *Baptism and Fullness*, Inter Varsity Press, 1977, pp.114–115.

6. Alfred Kuen,*Die charismatische Bewegung*, (*The Charismatic Movement*, translated), Brockhaus Verlag Wuppertal, p.55.

7. Grant Swank, *Christianity Today*, Feb. 28, 1975, p.13.

8. *Spiritual Renewal* edited by Frank Holmes, Quest (Western) Publications, 1977, p.82.

9. William MacDonald, *1.Korintherbrief*, (*1st Corinthians*, translated) 1971, pp.150–151).

10. Michael Griffiths, *Three men filled with the Spirit*, p.41.

11. John Stott, *Your Mind Matters*, Inter Varsity Fellowship, 1972, pp.27–28.

Quoting this famous theologian does not necessarily mean that I agree with everything else this author has stated. This is also true for other writers quoted as above.

12. John Stott, *Your Mind Matters.*

13. Spiros Zodhiates, *Tongues?!,* AMG Publishers, 1978, pp 22–23.

14. Michael Griffiths, *Three men filled with the Spirit,* p.31.

15. Ibid, p.21.

16. Merril Unger, *What Demons Can Do to Saints,* pp.164 and 168.

17. *Spiritual Renewal,* p.41.

18. Dennis Bennett, *Nine o'clock in the Morning,* Kingsway Publications Ltd. Eastbourne, E. Sussex 1987, pp.43–44.

19. George E. Gardiner, *The Corinthian Catastrophe,* Kregel Publications, Grand Rapids, 1976, p.11.

20. Johannes Greber, *Der Verkehr mit der Geisterwelt* (*Communication with the Spirit World,* translated), Brunner Verlag, 1937, p.133.

21. Quoted by Roy Livesey in *Understanding Deception,* New Wine Press, 1987, pp.2–3.

22. Spiros Zodhiates, *Tongues?!,* pp.22–23.

23. Arnold Bittlinger, *Glossolalia,* Rolf Kuehne Verlag, 1966, p.26.

24. Watchman Nee, *The Spiritual Man,* Christian Fellowship Publishers, Inc., New York, Vol. 3, 1968, p.119.

25. Kathryn Kuhlman, *Nothing is Impossible With God,* Prentice Hall, The Englewood Cliffs, New Jersey 1974, p 192, translated.

26. *Revival Report,* No. 6/82, p.15 and No. 3/4, p.3.

27. Dave Hunt *CIB Bulletin,* January 1992, Vol. 8, No. 1.

28. *Christianity Today,* July 1987, p.50.

29. Demos Shakarian, *The Happiest People on Earth,* by John and Elizabeth Sherill, Hodder and Stoughton, p.39.

30. John Wimber, verbatim quotation from a tape.

31. Lile Murphy, *Beginning at Topeka,* quoted in *Calvary Review,* Spring 1974, Volume XIII, p.4.

32. John Stott, *Baptism and Fullness,* p.56.

33. G.H. Lang, *The Earlier Years of the Modern Tongues Movement,* 1958, p.9.

34. Ibid, pp.28–29.

35. *Wort + Geist, (Word + Spirit),* December 1973, p 13.

36. R.A.Torrey, *Is the Present 'Tongues' Movement of God?* leaflet, The Biola Book Room, California.

37. Gerhard Wissmann, *Jesus — Nachfolge oder Jesus — Trip,* unpublished but circulated article, p.29.

38. Hank Hanegraaff, *Christianity in Crisis,* Harvest House Publishers, 1993, p.334.

39. Dave Hunt, *The Seduction of Christianity,* Harvest House Publishers, 1986, p.20. Hunt mainly quotes from Cho's *The Fourth Dimension,* Logos, 1979.

40. Ibid, p.102 and 111.

41. Ibid, pp.113–114.

42. Ibid, p.78.

43. Agnes Sanford, *Healing Light,* p.154.

44. Dave Hunt, p.139.

45. Ibid, p.143.

46. *Christianity Today,* "Big Trouble at the World's Largest church," January 22, 1982, p.39.

47. David W. Cloud, *O Timothy,* Vol. 4, Issues 8–9, 1987.

48. *Erneuerung in Kirche und Gesellschaft, (Renewal in church and Society,* translated), No. 7, 1980, p.26.

49. *CZB, Impuls,* translated, No. 5/81.

50. Roland Buck, *Angels on Assignment* by Charles and Francis Hunter, Leuchter-Verlag, 1980, p.61, translated.

51. Wilson Ewin, *The Spirit of Pentecostal Charismatic Unity,* Bible Baptist church, Nashua, p.18.

52. John Stott, *Your Mind Matters,* pp.10–11.

53. Leonhard Ravenhill, *Why Revival Tarries,* Send the Light Trust, 1975, p.3.

54. Peter Wagner, *Territorial Spirits and World Missions,* Evangelical Missions Quarterly, Vol. 25, No. 3, July 1989, pp.283–284.

55. Ibid, p.284.

56. John H. Armstrong, *In Search of Spiritual Power,* edited by Michael Horton, Power Religion, Moody Press, 1992, p.64 and pp.68–69.

57. Ibid, p.68.

58. Stanley Burgess and Bary McGee, *Dictionary of Pentecostal and Charismatic Movements,* Regency, 1988, p.161.

59. Hank Hanegraaff, *Christianity in Crisis,* p.353.

60. Arnold Bittlinger, *Integrating Other Religious Traditions into Western Christianity,* published in *Spirituality in Interfaith Dialoque,* edited by Tosh Arai and Wesley Ariarajah, Geneva, World Council of churches Publications, 1989, p.96–97.

61. Wallace Slater, *The Theosophist,* Sept. 1980, p.561.

ABOUT THE AUTHOR

Alexander Seibel was born in Vienna in 1943. Brought up in normal religious setting, he later discarded his faith and became an atheist. His main interest as a student were the subjects of science.

During his student days, it was through the testimony of Christians of a world-wide American missionary movement that he was confronted with the Gospel and the Bible.

What brought about the change in his mind was the evident fulfillment of Biblical prophecies in relation to Israel. The final breakthrough came through a message about true discipleship. It was the 4th of August, 1968 when he surrendered his life to the Lord Jesus Christ.

Till the completion of his studies, he was a member of a Baptist church in Vienna. Alexander Seibel, who holds a Masters of Technology, now works as a full-time evangelist. He speaks on the subjects of science, the Bible and evolution or creation to youth groups and students.

Mr. Seibel has engaged in an extensive study of the Charismatic Movement and recent trends in our society and churches. He has authored several books, some of them up to five editions, which have been translated into several European languages.

Alexander Seibel now lives in Germany, is married and the father of three children.

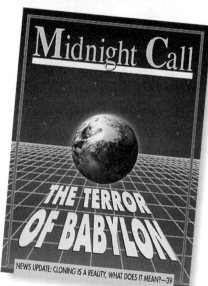

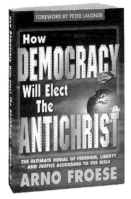

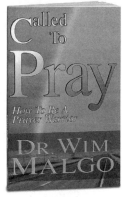